THE WORLD COMPARED

TO A BUBBLE

‿ BOOKS, CHAPBOOKS & COLLABORATIONS BY ANNE WALDMAN

On the Wing

O My Life!

Giant Night

Baby Breakdown

No Hassles

West Indies Poems

Life Notes

Self-Portrait (with Joe Brainard)

Fast Speaking Woman

Memorial Day (with Ted Berrigan)

Journals & Dreams

Sun the Blonde Out

Shaman / Shamane

Polar Ode (with Eileen Myles)

Countries

Cabin

First Baby Poems

Sphinxeries (with Denyse Du Roi)

Makeup on Empty Space

Invention (with Susan Hall)

Skin Meat Bones

The Romance Thing

Den Monde in Farbe Sehen

Blue Mosque

Tell Me About It: Poems for Painters

Helping the Dreamer: New &
  Selected Poems

Her Story (with Elizabeth Murray)

Not a Male Pseudonym

Lokapala

Fait Accompli

Troubairitz

Iovis: All Is Full of Jove

Kill or Cure

Iovis II

La Donna Che Parla Veloce

Au Lit/Holy (with Eleni Sikelianos
  & Laird Hunt)

Young Manhattan (with Bill Berkson)

Polemics (with Anselm Hollo &
  Jack Collom)

Homage to Allen G. (with George
  Schneeman)

Kin (with Susan Rothenberg)

One Voice in Four Parts
  (with Richard Tuttle)

Marriage: A Sentence

Zombie Dawn (with Tom Clark)

Dark Arcana/Afterimage or Glow

In the Room of Never Grieve:
  New & Selected Poems

Fleuve Flâneur (with Mary Kite)

STRUCTURE OF
THE WORLD COMPARED
TO A BUBBLE

ANNE WALDMAN

PENGUIN POETS

PENGUIN BOOKS
Published by the Penguin Group
Penguin Group (USA) Inc., 375 Hudson Street, New York, New York 10014, U.S.A.
Penguin Group (Canada), 10 Alcorn Avenue, Toronto, Ontario, Canada M4V 3B2
(a division of Pearson Penguin Canada Inc.)
Penguin Books Ltd, 80 Strand, London WC2R 0RL, England
Penguin Ireland, 25 St Stephen's Green, Dublin 2, Ireland (a division of Penguin Books Ltd)
Penguin Group (Australia), 250 Camberwell Road, Camberwell, Victoria 3124, Australia
(a division of Pearson Australia Group Pty Ltd)
Penguin Books India Pvt Ltd, 11 Community Centre, Panchsheel Park, New Delhi - 110 017, India
Penguin Group (NZ), cnr Airborne and Rosedale Roads, Albany, Auckland, New Zealand
(a division of Pearson New Zealand Ltd)
Penguin Books (South Africa) (Pty) Ltd, 24 Sturdee Avenue, Rosebank, Johannesburg 2196, South Africa

Penguin Books Ltd, Registered Offices:
80 Strand, London WC2R 0RL, England

First published in Penguin Books 2004

1   3   5   7   9   10   8   6   4   2

Copyright © Anne Waldman, 2004
All rights reserved

Page ix constitutes an extension of this copyright page.

Illustrations by Lucille Yap on pages 10 and 49 and other drawings from *Borobudur: Golden Tales of the Buddhas* by John Miksic (Periplus Editions, 1990) are used with permission.

LIBRARY OF CONGRESS CATALOGING IN PUBLICATION DATA
Waldman, Anne, 1945–
Structure of the world compared to a bubble / Anne Waldman.
p.   cm.
ISBN 0 14 30.3420 0
1. Buddhist poetry, American.   I. Title
PS3573.A4215S77 2004
811'.54—dc22   2004044580

Printed in the United States of America
Set in Bembo
Designed by Ginger Legato

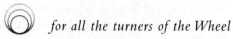 *for all the turners of the Wheel*

That I am a singer of little songs,
  Proves that I have learned to read the world as a book.

—Milarepa

so that, living within,
  you beget, self-out-of-self,

selfless,
  that pearl of great price.

—H. D.
from "The Walls Do Not Fall"

Acknowledgments

Milarepa quote from *Technicians of the Sacred,* Editor: Jerome Rothenberg, University of California Press, Berkeley, California.

With gratitude to the Civitella Ranieri Center, Umbria, Italy, to the Naropa University Study Abroad Programs, Boulder/Bali, and to the Foundation for Contemporary Performance Arts for support and time to work on this book.

A page of this text was first published in *The Poetry Project Newsletter.*

And with gratitude to my Buddhist teachers the Dorje Dradul and Jadtral Rinpoche whose teachings grace these pages.

Thanks also to my editor at Penguin, Paul Slovak, and to my husband Ed Bowes for their ongoing perspicacity, and to Ambrose Bye, always.

Contents

A Vajradhatu or "Diamond World" mandala, based on a ninth-century Tibetan version.

The magnificent stupa of Borobudur in Java, Indonesia, is an architectural provocation. It begs numerous questions, and seems to be a still-active container as well as a mandala or diagram of an advanced philosophy that invites a spiritual and psychological voyage for the visitor.

The stupa form originated in pre-Buddhist India as a burial tumulus or mound of earth surmounted by a wooden pillar symbolizing the frission between heaven, earth, and the underworld. The pole was seen as an energizing conductor, an antennae for a power spot that might benefit both the environment and those who witnessed it. The historical Buddha, it is said, requested to be buried under a stupa. After his cremation his ashes were placed under eight stupas at different places associated with principal events of his life. As a burial marker or reliquary the stupa then becomes a site of respect and spiritual practice. Stupas might also have commemorated particular sacred events, or have been constructed by wealthy rulers or patrons to gain religious merit. Ancient stupas are found in Java and other parts of Indonesia as well as India, Tibet, Nepal, and now in Europe, Canada, and America—places where Buddhism is flourishing—on a decidedly more modest scale than Borobudur. Yet the recently completed Great Stupa of Dharmakaya in Red Feather Lakes, Colorado—built with cement to last at least a thousand years—is a remarkably complex and stunning achievement. The pyramids of Egypt and Central and South America come to mind as resonant sites of power and influence that often honor a ruler or king, in addition to the ziggurats of Mesopotamia. The most spectacular religious monuments of the third millennium B.C.E. are the impressive ziggurats, a best preserved example being the ziggurat of the moon goddess Nanna at Ur (in what is contemporary Iraq). Height and a feeling of aspiration—ascension—has been associated with religious edifices for centuries. It was this particular upward spiritual motion at Borobudur that inspired the writings of this book.

Designed as both mandala or psychological map for the Buddhist pilgrim, as well as a spiritual challenge to the curious layperson or secular aesthete, Borobudur was built on a hill that sits on Java's lush Kedu plain. It has a long and complex history and was almost lost until its "discovery" in the nineteenth century, a process which took over fifty years, instigated in part by Lieutenant-Governor Thomas Stanford Raffles, the first colonial ruler to take an interest in Javanese antiquities and history. Raffles, an unusual colonialist employee, being both scholar and writer, dispatched H.C. Cornelius, a Dutch engineer, to the ruin, which took a month and half for two hundred men to uncover. It had been piled high with dirt and overgrown with centuries of thick vegetation. Subsequent staggered recovery and reconstruction took many years.

Buddhism enjoyed only a short period of popularity in central Java and was less practiced than Hinduism. This radical atheistic tradition had been introduced from India to China along the famed Silk Route in the first century C.E. Later a sea-link was forged between India and China, opened up by Indonesian sailors who had several centuries of experience in maritime trade with other parts of Southeast Asia and India. Buddhist pilgrims traveled through the archipelago with increased frequency during the seventh and eighth centuries. Java and Sumatra were major centers of international Buddhist scholarship during this expansive cross-cultural period.

Buddhism was linked to the Sailendra—or "Lords of the Mountain"—family, which for a century supported Buddhist monuments and study in Java. Most likely construction of Borobudur began in 760 C.E. and was completed about 830. It is made up of some million stones hauled up from a nearby riverbed, weighing one hundred kilograms each. This required enormous manpower. Evidence indicates that the majority of workers were farmers and part-time artisans. They carved the reliefs, plastered and painted the final monument. Clearly material support and stimulus came from the Sailendra ruler of the time, but the workers were in no way slaves to the project. Archeological evidence shows that a strong community of laymen and women as well as "clergy" lived in Borobudur's environs and were inspired by the task at hand for several generations. Questions remain as to why the temple was nearly abandoned within seventy years of its completion, although there are records of inhabitation and some remains and pottery shards for subsequent years. Chinese porcelain shards have been found from the twelfth and thirteenth centuries, coins from the fourteenth. Yet no more temples were built in central Java after the beginning of the tenth century. It was not until the thirteenth century that a revival of stone construction began, taking place several hundred miles to the east of Borobudur. Did an an ominous volcanic eruption ("the sun became obscured, enveloped in a fog" are Raffles' words on an eruption that took place during his tenure, much later) obscure Borobudur or did the energy of trade and commerce move to coastal areas? Certainly the arrival of Islam in the fifteenth century challenged any remnants of Buddhist practice in the archipelago. Was there a sense of the stupa being built for the future to reclaim? This might be a more tantric idea: that an embryonic process goes on into the future, having a salutary effect on the citizens and the environment. And that these monuments are built with the "enlightenment" of future generations in mind. Certainly the current world situation would seem to belie this, given the destruction of the Bamiyan Buddhas by the Taliban in recent years and the tragic conflation of religious conflicts due to political, economic, and ideological power struggles.

But the legacy of Borobudur remains to my own visitor's eyes, reawakened and forcefully intact and perhaps a goad toward greater archival and artistic preservation of all cultures' rich remains. "I hunt among stones" was poet Charles Olson's line. The ignominious disregard for such treasures during times of war needs corrective.

Most powerful at this site perhaps is the narrative sequence of reliefs carved into the million stones, narratives which teach a spiritual, gentle, and harmonious way of life. The reliefs are arranged so that as one ascends the stupa the stories turn complicated and abstract, much as Dante's *Paradiso* becomes less tangible in its language and more fixated on the play of light and the purity of the notion of love as free from worldly attachment. The progress of the pilgrim is a symbolic progression from the "world of illusion" or dream to one of knowledge and enlightenment, "enlightenment"—a state of existence which essentially means being "awake" and beyond the grasping of individual ego. Buddha literally means the "awakened one" and it is assumed that other human beings might have the same aspiration to break out of the wheel of perpetual suffering—*samsara*—through spiritual practice and commitment to a life in the service of other beings. *Putting others before oneself.* This is known as the Mahayana—the Middle Way—the path of the Bodhisattva. Thus Borobudur is essentially an image of the world according to the Buddhism of the Mahayana.

A hidden foot at the base of the stupa—later covered by a design revision—illustrates the principles of cause and effect through moral tales. Lively carvings depict heroic deeds, the *Jataka Tales* (past lives of the Buddha) and *Avadanas* (heroic deeds), and two *sutras* or teaching-texts: the *Lalitavistara* or "The Unfolding of the Play," which is literally about the *performance* of the Buddha in the world, and the *Gandavyuha* or "The Structure of the World Compared to a Bubble," from which this poem takes its title. These enable the pilgrim to read the monument pictorially *as a book*. This Gandavyuha is considered the most important text—in the category of a third level tantra. It follows the pilgrim Sudhana—a kind of everyman—as he travels through a series of encounters (with a rabbit, a rock, a mythical female creature, the future Buddha Maitreya) that manifest in the phenomenal world as teacher. Again, there is a sense of ascending through lower realms to higher levels of realization and psychological understanding. Issues and examples of cause and effect (*karma*), the transitory quality of our existence, suffering generated by self-induced styles of psychological imprisionment, in particular the Tibetan Buddhist notion of "jealous (or warring) god realm," "charnel ground," and the path of the Bodhisattva through ten stages are explored in the writing as it weaves in, out of and around these themes. Statues also line the route of the winding monument. There are 432 Buddha statues on five balustrades of the lower levels, all exhibiting particular and significant hand mudras (gestures), and seventy-two statues on the round terraces at the top which sit inside bell-spaced stupas—or "cages" as they are popularly called—of their own. In order to follow the complete narrative sequence of the reliefs from beginning to end, the pilgrim has to make ten circuits of the stupa—four times around the first gallery and twice around each of the next three galleries. Ten is also the number of stages in the career of the Bodhisattva, with an eleventh "bhumi" factored in for good measure when the being actually *becomes* a Bodhisattva. It is reckoned that the whole process in walking around the galleries of the stupa—if done properly—is equivalent to five kilometers.

I view this serial poem as a range of lineaments—a walking meditation, a "cultural intervention," a sutra of mind, "recovery" of a sacred site, as a kind of *doha,* or religiously didactic poem, or as *dbangs* or *mgur,* which are compositions by scholars or priests in the Tibetan tradition, and a modern (or post-modern) "take" on contemporary reality—and how the busy "monkey-mind" (as it's called in Buddhism) works and travels. Invocation and mantra also have a role here. There was always the sense of the larger historical/cultural/religious aspects of the literal site. The poem ends on a boat.

Indonesia is primarily a Muslim country. An acquaintance in India, himself a practitioner of Islam, once remarked, "Of course, you know, Islam is the most *modern* religion," a notion I instantly grasped as both true and ironic. Modern because it perhaps has vast appeal for the disenfranchised. Modern because it has a strong immediately practical side—a moral code. I was struck by the generosity of the Muslim "container" and charmed by the hordes of youth who flock to the stupa daily as part of their religious/cultural study. They proudly claim the stupa as their own. A key for me is the notion of "syncretic"— both historically, as we sift through the remnants of powerful cultures, and contemporarily in the details of our own particular existence, experiencing the fluid layers and participation of cultures, realities, energies at work *all the time.* I spent several days with a Christian Javanese friend en route to the stupa; atop the monument itself I had some joyous times with these gaggles of young Muslim students. My informants primarily have been Tibetan Buddhist teachers.

This project began seminally with a trip to the Borobudur stupa in 1997 and continued in subsequent brief trips to Indonesia. I worked with the Naropa University's Study Abroad Program over the years (in Bali), and among other interests pursued gamelan music, which plays a part in the "cosmology" of this piece. Some of the carvings at Borobudur depict gamelan instruments in use at the time. Gamelan—a term which refers to a whole ensemble of metallophone instruments (with attendant drums and flutes)—is a music of circular, repeating melodic cycles. Its regenerative structures echo the circumambulatory practices and themes implicit in the carved "sutras" of Borobudur. Thus a presence of gongs provides emphasis, marks time, indicates pause, and invites an element of "performance" to the text. It is disheartening that the Indonesia program has had to be discontinued temporarily (as have other Naropa programs in Nepal and India) because of the ongoing political situation: intractable religious conflict stirred up by all "sides," forms of aggressive extremism and terrorism, hegemonic policies of my own empirical war-making country, which continue to fan the flames of anti-Western sentiment, the endless and relentless propagation of weaponry worldwide by the Masters of War. Hopefully this will change.

Obviously ongoing Buddhist studies are also relevant here, as Buddhist philosophy examines closely the root causes of suffering and the propagation of aggression and ignorance in ourselves and the world—the enemy is within, ultimately. We seem to constantly project and hallucinate demons and create more chaos by not looking into our own grasping and negativity. The Borobudur stupa provided a structure—and I believe that is its intention—by which to contemplate these things. I make no claims for being any the wiser, but I would like to dedicate whatever merit there is in this writing to the benefit of others.

STRUCTURE OF
THE WORLD COMPARED
TO A BUBBLE

startle of
in-the-sun-ruin becomes
    luminous
just so the whole of real life you
have no fear. . . . .
    walk in *pilgrimage*

    plangent fear ho

ah hum!

look up—a wide universe

            wings at your back, twinge
    quick to sweet love
pervades *samsara*
    wheel of suffering titled endless, call it
eternal, name it umitigated
                        or
    a way to interpret our
    particulate world
    mind creates
            a movie   an engine,   sprocket or
        gyre   or how
    to wake up beyond the identity kit dragged
    across town and into the forest
            beyond   last border crept by
    or prison if it comes to that

        must we?   drag?   climb too?

in cave:
        flashlight   water   soporific tablets
        twine

for practical wrapping,
    maybe allow one pencil
        to swift emergency, supply side
gets needed like opposite of sleek weaponry
    philosophical readiness for the best worst case century
or worst best cure maybe a celestial citing scenario
a flyby theory that nanotechnology is
        your next best worst good friend & gets you there
      or in the valley now you walk in a foreign land
          & your friend is "lineage" is "book" is "thinking"
    is the bleat of poetry

    is dawn of a somber age

    will you hear me out?

not the deal but way *of* the deal I said
like a wheel
(it doesn't have to be that negative version
    you could stop their cutting logs for . . .
  just one instinct . . .

playful or hush hum of machinery another "instanter" upon
        & fevered sense of unreality a third rush
sets in
    the "ah" hesitates to a swallowed revere—all-minimum
    so if one didn't hear correctly
it was said

    existence of suffering (1) ◎

    origin of suffering (2) ◎

    end of suffering (3) ◎

    complemented by

path (4) which is the way out you

 move

were   all true
    the first time I thought
    move   or   mutter mantra?
a meaning of meaning could be
    mosaics?
& in four parts taken?
    or gaze, fragmented
that things fluid change meaning or range to what
 meaning they are not and keep going in meaning
 as meanings do

as is the key to a message I color of
because much a fool

        & nothing lasts
 but makeup come off now

            color being high blush and waning

then there's real markup
 deathless   unborn   unchanging

in deflection   in shadow in   dissolve

            path rolls in under your feet

                                as is said

Prologue (with 108 Gongs)

[walking towards the imaginal and literal site
which is here, thumping on head & heart]

◎ It was in the middle of my life I read the world as a
◎ book—faded gold stone dramas meticulous wind
◎ which parts are doctrinal on the one hand
◎ and then you are free to live and interpret as you will
◎ a philosophy gathered here on a million blocks of stone
◎ that's to say relevant to say I won't
◎ get shuttled or shoved by fear again
◎ denied in catastrophic *nuit, noche, notte*
◎ night and whatever extra bite for Javanese-Sanskrit sounding
◎ theme—doth bring—calendar? cosmology? wake-up call?
◎ no one can keep you from the stupa gate
◎ collective civilization brings in love or
◎ destroys itself in conflict and kinship reckonings
◎ care is *Huan* and *Human* both and told this by
◎ biccolage or off the French cuff, theoretical philosophers'
◎ gloom or sound oft foiled by threat then
◎ swims out of erotics full of war
◎ a breeze blowing towards the land
◎ towards a charnel ground of death
◎ syntagmy of aether of appropriate time and place
◎ of lines never drawn, roads not buoyed
◎ but trawl a bit, cast a net for the others
◎ from Middle Dutch *traghelen,* to drag
◎ travel far, not a pilgrim that does not travel
◎ thy medium loving in the direction of propagation
◎ the ice breaks, you are once again at sea and holy
◎ pneumatically sealed on your bodhisattva path
◎ air gets in the interstices you want to escape
◎ from while you are in an act of cross-fading
◎ not a revealed religion but a walk on a wildebeeste side
◎ you might survey your life from here, does it resemble
◎ the himalayan flower, the spikenard, a devout seeker?
◎ does it resemble a book with no titular readiness
◎ exposed to terror of horrible magnitude

◎ a book that's *sans* words—is that it?
◎ humectant person on the fertile plain
◎ delirious, the morning is delirious you are
◎ relegated to the lower animal realm
◎ rein in the doubts with your absent books your absent resolve
◎ nothing unjust, nothing to declare: what's the fear?
◎ go up—approach the wall from your armored mental-citadel
◎ walls have ears in the desert—they feel your fear
◎ offer a *patois* here a patina of humility
◎ offer a more spiffy conscious self come from Manahatta isle
◎ offer a *canzonetta* a song from Italia
◎ offer a territory containing the capital of a country
◎ offer flowers and incense
◎ offer the mistral, the master wind
◎ offer the female complement to a breeze
◎ offer your bluestocking ways
◎ offer the arcane when you are tempted to
◎ dismantle the impervious system
◎ when you want to destroy yourself and others
◎ offer sounds that ululate that make a clamour
◎ offer the interiors of the whole shell
◎ offer a linguistic conundrum to "pink" to "purple"
◎ graphology for a woman's hand is indicated
◎ the woman's desire to get there first: offer
◎ poetry that makes a grinding sound easy to offer
◎ that mimics the orality of the sounds-like-a-can-opener bird
◎ think of Greek graptos i.e. "marked with letters"
◎ no *gran turismo* on the Kedu Plain but
◎ a way to die if it comes to that
◎ linguistics of blame are here to remind
◎ you a range of being exists greatly agitated
◎ a state of grace in which you grasp naught but darkness
◎ nothing pontifical but a "heart that sighs"

◎ nothing political but "ends and means"
◎ riding over storms of old age sickness and death
◎ the precise nature of your suffering alludes you
◎ the *nidana* chain: its links of the cause and effect allude you
◎ elucidate the old woman's potter's wheel
◎ the *keffiyeh* of migrations of suffering
◎ will sign your name in blood
◎ circumambulate the monument ten times
◎ palm leaves and other perishables are offered
◎ gold plates might hold an inscription
◎ devised for commoners such as you are
◎ not priests abound it says if you, commoner,
◎ can break the seal—cut it now!
◎ a verse to honor Queen Sri Kahuluan
◎ a verse to benefit the company of women
◎ a verse to benefit the spallation of our nuclei
◎ a verse for poor Mary, a verse for St. Catherine
◎ a verse for St. Elizabetta
◎ a verse for the tumulus they lie under
◎ a verse for those under religious persecution
◎ a verse for the indica of words and prayers
◎ a verse for the signees of this humane decree
◎ a verse for a Brocken spectre
◎ that indicates stance amongst cloud-rainbow-mountain
◎ for the latest broadcast so you don't worry its condescension
◎ from the steering committee so you don't fret
◎ a verse to check your weapons at the gate . . . . . . but will you?
◎ a verse to conjure the realms of existence
◎ a voice to conjure a sense of purpose
◎ a verse to conjure lion, jaguar, garuda, dragon
◎ a voice that sounds like wailing mothers
◎ a verse to conjure *dakas* and *dakinis*
◎ a verse to conjure spirit guides for the traveler

a verse to invite speculation
◎ a verse to honor all the great philosophers
◎ a verse errant, allowing the tenacious urban myth
◎ a Kabbalist verse you all learned in school—turbaned?
◎ a zodiacal light left hanging as you look into the mirror of your mind
◎ a verse to chant as you walk and contemplate your good fortune here
◎ inside a crazy world system gone mad with suffering
◎ a *Dies Irae* consisting of all these whirling worlds

   (radiant and louder gongs at end)

Walking out of Six Styles of Imprisionment

hell realm (scalding to seek revenge, or else cold, locked in an ice missile)

- ◎ Reviving Hell
- ◎ Black-line Hell
- ◎ Crushing, Howling Hells
- ◎ Great Howling Hell
- ◎ Heating Hell
- ◎ Intense Heating Hell
- ◎ Hell of Ultimate Torment
- ◎ Hell of Blisters
- ◎ Teeth-Chattering Hell
- ◎ Lamentations Hell
- ◎ Hell of Lotus Cracks

Caught now in lamentable aggression. Mind can't sleep with an unstable "she" in the wings. Send this, wake this, read this, stalk this, ride this. Incandescent rage of "she" of "her." Presume nothing is ever heard she doesn't hear to make her ride harder. Hair trigger away: to pop off like that. Ride harder then hear her own echo more than enough to fill all the universes and their echoes. Ride, ride *her*. And harder. Scant glimmer of other—image, object, person of other "I"s, other sapiens in their bright colors. With skin and hair and eyes. With incandescent desire, the first light of desire and rage. Accoutrements of all kinds. Flames and Kalasnikovs. She was "right" to ride to stalk to profiteer all anger. Have to be right. Had to had to. Right over them ride. Her plight to be a riddle of anger, a lozenge of anger hard in the throat. Sword in the throat. Projectile war. To be coughed up. Project an enraged face or dart from a star, a new concept in attack. Project torture as in *I will get you with your fear I will I will*. To the ends of earth a grimace. All the universe with a black cloud mind, a huge simulacrum of grimace. She once projects degradation because it serves the fuel to make enemy of you. Investiture in being right, mercifully right. About all of them a right wing of revenge best beat down on you. Can you feel her better-than-your heat? Hotter-than-your hell? Feel her cold—cooler-than-your breath? The earth she witnesses now like fire, turns next towards air and suffocation. Everyone else was the enemy. We are in the right, she said, triumphant before the image of her glory crumbled, was to crumble. All sides of it to make a royal "we" the better to be right against "you" with. She was stifled in magnificent aggression never to crumble, she thought. I am right about the weather, what it is doing, the quality of day, the mysteries of the night, the sensible opinion to have. I am right about the decision to go or not to go, the decision of where to go, the decision of never going at all. Never having gone. Awake in it all right, all the night. All of my "I"s become the multiple "We" in speaking for all of you. All options are mine to be right with. I have a right to them and to my righteous anger. Image of glory, is it really an image? Hardly. A flag. A chimera. Something bickering flickers. No more image than this: of being deep inside the earth—crushed down—encircled on all rough sides. Unable to look up afraid the world caves in on you. What kind of cloud is that? Cirrus? A fear cloud? A mushroom cloud? Where are the mushroom star wars? Where is the favored planet Jupiter? Where is the red Mars planet of war we land upon to wreck its havoc for more war plans? Why am I in the echo of my own, her own mind? My own disarray? Alone. No "we" to bolster up the economy. But firm in this. Alone and Up against It. Needing this. They, the enemy, she conjectures, is loose upon the world. Upon the universe. Hatred for that universe. Hatred for that enemy. Theories of malleable string, of black holes, ride free and trap me. They run the show of her hatred. I hate all those theories who run my show. They brought me to this sorrow and are the cause of sorrow. They do not tell me in my sorrow who I am who we are, why we are here. They brought me to this humiliation. To this anger that wants to harm, to burn and ride. They fill up the premises and the sky is thick with purple clouds of sickness. Under a line of palpable fire. Undermined. I now put them in my line of fire. Could be any-where. Crowded boxcar. Open prairie. Furnace. Solitary retreat hut. Immigra-tion camp. Holding tank. Another mountain entirely. Or by the sea. Many erogenous zones of libation and sexuality. Many temporary zones of control and deprivation. Held down by a nameless one, pinned down by sorrowful name of "anger." Held down by the oppressor pronoun of anger. Who listens? oblivious in their "me, me" distractions—of job, religion, engrossing book, other secret love affair, business, greed, game, maintenance of torture. I am the ignorant abused neglected frothing powerless shrieking scalding one. Seeking revenge with my Iron Hammer, with my Red Dawn. Thrown down from many stories, many heights. Then there's He. Or there's a She. Or there's a They. He/She/They tricked me. He is the absolute one to blame. He—that one, that one was the one. That other one who made me what I am: full of anger. He—that man—who put me here. And kept me here full of anger to burn. She too, putting me here, reducing me to be here, under here. Angry because they are more beautiful—those others—more intelligent, more powerful. Stuck in a place where all the lights go out. No recourse to myself. Hating myself. Shamed by my horrible need. Need for light. For water. For shelter. Stuck in the hospital with an IV in arm. Aches all the more thinking of "stuck like this." Stuck in the madhouse. Who is listening? Nailed down. Little blue thing. Small purple thing. Nailed. Small red furious thing. Others out there in their freedom going about the day no impunity. Hate they might be laughing. They are not like me up against the flames, not like me inside their troubling gender (which one? which one?). Not inside their troubling clothes. Not inside their troubling habits. Not inside their troubled monkey-mind. Hot in here, trapped in the troubling heat. Ditches of burning coals. Swamps filled with rotting corpses. Highways paved with razorblades. Shadows of other realms cycle through my mind. Adrift in rivers of roiling, boiling water or maybe locked in a pillar of ice. Maybe earth is frozen iron. Impenetrable meteoric iron. She, the other one of me, seems so cold. He does not embrace me the other one of me as he once did and now seems so cold. The willpowers that run these scenarios of hell—hot & cold— are misguided other ones of me who is both hot and cold. Corridors I will tell you of chance operation. Corridors I will tell you of corridors with no way out. What is it to be upended? To be lost. I am looking at myself: Ice Maiden. Cold to the touch. Turn me over. If I blame you torturers do I blame myself? Look in the glass. Gambit, palace, governance. What is the image on the screen. Vacant. Passive. Who invented it? Self-serving. Condescending. Provocative. Down with their empire. Ticking off the news of the day with no heart. No heart inside their words, inside their little increments of talk and groan. Of banter. I am ticking in time-bomb-anger, ready to explode. Harm to you who harms me. I make you up and *dis* you again, again. No grasp of how you sound, how I sound. Nothing heard in grasping so hard. Ice my tongue! It burns . . . lash out.

You'd told this pilgrimage-story fractured
A prologue fractured by its own lit-up remorse
A language twisted in her turn of remorse: hell realm
As if there was a way to go back on something
Blatantly sealed, a Canopic jar, say
Or canister of tear gas
A moratorium of ecclesiastical religion
Which this isn't, sighting the "passing show"
Sighting that there is no god on the premises so why
Invent him? An enemy?
She who was bound by desire to make no small talk
Was to get in gear to save something beyond her own hide
Is that the duty of a saint?
Getting "realer" What could that be,
skins of all beautiful lovers?
And for whom?
The land here is fertile,
keep up the gait
Revulsion is the foot of meditation, as is said
Then glory-sounding beyond remorse
A place hard to get to, pilgrim, kept walking
In hot day walk the scorching miles
Words that could fray or join the task
OM MANE PADME HUM
In syncretic dance, in syncretic salutation
My Hebrew Aleph my Arabic twain of twin
My old Etruscan tongue, dark stubble
My coming to hear inside a Muslim land
A dharma song, hip to still be lovin' you oh people
Yet we cry out "water! water!"
We cry out innumerable epithets
Is not that the miserable human method?
Roots of the first song that leads to an architectural mystery

Down a forbidden path extolling passionate words in sexual collusion
That told me how to live on the ascending rock
Pictures that sound names
That depict My Everyman My Everywoman
Every possible gender construct
What the pandits name "bhumis" meaning levels,
Grounds of details, of daily-ness, working up to abstracts
Is it ever clear that you could categorize a state of mind
The official position compartmentalizes itself to
"I have a mind of winter," or a mind in the gutter
Some wind sweeps leaves at her feet
Her mind grasped the next moment: I have it here, look!
And do you? A ramble
So turned to precious Dharma-Stone-Narrative here
Far from home, exile for the asking
You swept the core resistance, stubbornly alone
Alert as the man who came to your bungalow
You need a massage madam? Entertain a thought
Of need, rise at dawn, the sun behind you
While twin statues elsewhere might collapse into dust
You blamed an enemy, who else?
And bow, keep bowing, your hands then
Raise in supplication
The Muslim way
Elbows at sides, forearms extending outward
Palms open to heaven, anyone up there watching?
See me in my need?
Then betoken the bucolical way of need in paint
Then betoken a way to sing of this
Your chords on fire like a martyr Christian

Sex-chords on fire like a holy prostitute
What is the difference between a prostitute
And a drug user? & macho misogyny (she washes her crack etc. . . .)
Like anguish of any tortured religion
Self-immolation by monks during war of Vietnam
All roads lead away from theistic god
But toward a mind that might accomplish most
Inroads toward Mecca
Cheek, take it on the cuff instead . . .
Babe you know my name
Lover, let me go—to martyrdom
rub your self with other or taste the drip of instillation
Barrd from Celtic wants origin
She wants a reason to believe in words
Will they last? Pass on?
Were not gentle beasts believed to be and
Toughness of the dream a bard or book
You blame migratory routes
Rapid deceitful talk Eve moves even more into
You blame a straying glance, innuendo, a rib
You blame extreme unction, the extreme of extremes
You blame the *reliquiae*
The happy idiot *worship of idols*
You blame the throngs of heathens
Stuck on self-love, consuming 'til they
Bloat, necks wither in the Hungry Ghost realm
You blame the Warring Gods, caught in mutual hallucination
Armed in righteousness
You blame the hedonists lost in pleasure of cunt and cock
You blame all the surcharges, added daily
To the obligatory "bill"

hungry ghost realm (avid on the scent of your own sweet appetite)

She was restless toward insatiable motor desire. Take her there. Appetite for pleasure, food, shiny acquisitions. The more she craves the hungrier she grows. Come into a mouth, feed the swollen belly. Belly: perpetually starved. Belly of greed. Come things, come external world of things, come inside me to make me exist. Lust for you . . . things—save all my lust for you. Sometimes I see you raw, the flesh of you, the sex of you. Then "you" disappear inside "me," never gratified. Never full. Always empty. Hungry ghost a demon, like a vampire. Hungry ghost your own sweet appetite. Hunger is vast. Hunger gnaws upon itself so vast. Neither fully human nor fully animal but a tormented vast existence. Haunt, grasp, grab, appropriate a thought, appropriate a person. Want to buy and acquire all the accoutrements to make the self exist. Want to exist, as ever. Suspended here, caught here, as "preta," one departed, here to haunt— dead but hovering, unfulfilled—want more. Never enough. Want more. What could you possibly want? What would it take to make you say "enough." Desire is never satisfied. Make love to me, never sated, never enough. More of you, never enough. Absorb you, never enough. Never enough. How to find what I need. Never enough food, enough water. Starving as one might in Africa, in North Korea, in any pogrom (O daughters of Chechnya of Palestine!) in all the refugee camps of all the world, in all the inner tragic cities, in all the diasporas of the world. Long fingers will never take hold of what they reach for. The thing, that thing-to-be-grasped is an illusion, falls through itself. Subtle desire tortures the body. Then the mind inside feeding on itself, eating the brain, how horrible. Look out, never see. Notice? What? Throat is so small, and stomach so large. Hallucinate the food & drink as they burst into flames inside the body and burn from within. Sometimes turns into pus, blood, urine. Sometimes food becomes like iron. Iron avarice, iron stinginess, iron meanness. Scrimp, hoard, do you know the type? Conspicuous consumption, secret addiction. I never wear the clothes I have.

Beautiful objects hidden from view. Don't come near me with your inquisitiveness. No longer able to devour sensations with a hungry ghost mind yet how avid that flower that scent that next other attractive person. Like a *ghandarva* living off the scent of food, feeling pangs of hunger like a flesh and blood one, but only able to eat what sustenance has been dedicated, especially, earmarked. Fall in love again, again never settled never satisfied never resolved, never at ease. If only. . . . eternal seeker, restless in clothes, eternal student never knowing enough of epistomology, eternal con artist using people and situations to move along. If only . . . everything, everyone is an object for consumption. Like a blood-drinking nocturnal *rakshasa,* like a wraith on the fringe of the nuclear holocaust. Like the endless "once upon the world" denizens in their aftermath of destruction, ashen ghosts hovering confused above the cold burial ground. If only . . . avid for all the reminders of past success of wooing of winning of taking more things in stride of standing empty-handed of being naked in front of him for the first time of being tongue-tied but mouth open lusting for more of him to swallow, of inching down the body, ragged, ravenous clawing the body for sustenance. Hit the dirt now, squeeze plants for water, catch rain in wretched, bony hands, or go shop in eternity. How many shiny processed crisp wrapped-up stuff can you handle? How many more addenda to your life? How many things to hoard, shore up for the dark ages, how much more built in obsolete things that break down, won't work, won't move don't light up don't sing won't dance won't do the job won't last won't resolve the panic won't placate a broken heart won't be remembered won't disappear but leave traces of waste that will take thousands of years to disintegrate. She remembers the Hindu legend of Brahma who embodies the creative energy of desire. He created the first female—a mind-born daughter—with his tremendous mental powers. But because he was Brahma, the primordial god of desire, he felt inherent lust for her. He was also good, true, pure—but was he? other attributes of poor noble Brahma—ok, so he was conflicted. Brahma struggled to control his feeling. He yearned, he wants. He desires. Sweat pours and pours from his body as he fights to restrain himself. Hungry ghosts exit the pores of his body . . . Centuries pass without their hearing any mention of water.

Paid in full or in protracted pain?
Intense radiation
You blame the conflagration of ideology
Of sinister nationalisms
Where are the noble women?
And why are they always interrupted as they start to speak
That Eve you mentioned should be your verb
to remind and castigate to reprimand and placate
Ere she move like any old woman neglected
You have a place for her in your stones?
Any woman desire this
Pilgrim, you are woman!
Step lightly on these stones
Take off your veil now so you breathe
At fixed trine or place
A grand trine in fire guides you
At a rouse from sleep you dream
you were being seduced by a daughter of Mara the Tempter
Always called to account in speech saying "littler"
I was "littler" oh "littler"
Women buried alive for being widowed
With humble gaze
No, stand up to humility she says
Your taciturn nature turned to good account
A kind translation turned in pure amount
And this is not even War
And relish my gunpoint at dream
Enlightenment they speak of enlightenment
"Endarkenment" its kindly twin
Meant you can't trust? And soonest mended

Tell me, tell me: is the rift ever mended?
Translated it means "go on," keep a steady climb
Spasmodically, intermittently who had signs
Who had signs and consigned herself here
Illumined like a wimpled nun? Or the rest of
Us? the greedy us, mollusks of hat and shoulders of need
For approval, need of confirmation
Always another raving observation checking itself or
Galvanized to being epic: what if you aren't so good?
And a gambled deck is driven by speed and drama
A noble machine threshes in prone direction
Circulate clockwise until you spiral the top
Then bend sinister
So by walking there one enters the mind of votary
Paying homage is an artifact made by human beings
To light up their own minds
Reading its walls as moral code
You blame the other predators before yourself
Stupid ignorant mind that needed this one direction
Stupa which is monument of stone
Designed to wake you up to the nature—
I mean details—of self-existing equanimity
Insist on observance of formalities
Bow again to your own hawk-mind here
Its eyes are the eyes of search and destroy
I mean destruction of ego
Or resist this intrusion
Organized research in
The scholarly way of a buddha
System that thrives on nothing
That seeks nothing that says
You are here to disappear, poet

A bushwhacker might respond to a sentence here
Timed to matriculate a first cause
But some say "mandate," didn't Dante mention this?
Are you ready now to climb?
We are errant we are scared so we
Run to hide and reestablish
Rules of engagement
And are you author of such a book?
Risible in "suchness?"
Are you? Ready to examine your own mind?
Softened by love in its heat?
The way a fabric bends
Are you game? Or are you phony?
Are you on a quest?
Are you solvent in your escapades?
Do you eschew money laundering?
Have you maintained accountability?
Well bravo, I can speak to you
Soldiers of the throne
O you say they are stiff, corpses of the enemy
No, the tithing won't tire
A leer a tipsy insight
Round watch straps and manganese
The end of civilization ghosts all take seriously
Shifting their perspectives
Cell phones, it is reported in the dailies,
Are scaring all the ghosts away
Ghosts hungry for greater action

animal realm (to hunt to skin alive to wear upon a body)

on all fours mounted from behind, prey to a creature larger than i am. i am your
noble prey. these are the emotions of my existence: vulnerability, confusion.
subject to the law of the jungle. fear. bewilderment. hunger. what are the emo-
tions of the hunted of the preyed upon? it is like a dream where everything is a
manifestation of myself the animal-dreamer dreaming myself animal but instead
of beautiful animal—*protected, adored animal*—becoming animal that is hunted
animal besieged. everyone wants an animal in their lives. to hunt. to skin alive.
to wear on a body. to eat. to play with. every reference point is in the nature of
survival. food, shelter, affection. i am hidden, waiting. or abandoned made to
flourish and die later. as dreamer who sleeps on a dreamed of floor, dreamer
who sleeps on an apparent but dreamed of rug, animal who rages in a dreamed
of cage waiting for liberation: the world is narrowed down to my survival. wide
awake in ignorance needing to survive. killed or be killed is jungle law. never
lower your guard in an old testament law of the jungle. i am the holy predator
for you. i could mount your safari for you. constant paranoia. routines are
preferable. i know where i am when i eat. sleep. when someone comes to attend
me in my protected cat realm in my dog realm in my bird realm in my mink
realm in the realm of the marten the kookaberra the crustacean world of krill.
in the realm of the annelid. in the realm of *giraffa camelopardis* in my cheetah
realm, in the realm of the seal, the zoo of the seal, in the nest of the egret, in
the cave of the ice-white bear, in the cave of the bat, in the wild in the eu-
phemistic wild in the laborious wild in the endangered wild in the encroached-
upon-wild in the wild to be deliberated upon to be exploited in the courageous
wild in the relative wild in the avaricious wild in the unpredictable wild in the
wild of our ancestors in the wild of a war caught between realms of living and
of dead. in a glamorous wild in a wild of the imagination where everything is
bigger than life: the owl, the elephant. the buffalo. the dinosaur. the moose, the
wapiti, the mountain elk. the wild of the mourning dove the mourning cloak
the mourning warbler when everything was pristine and natural—remember?
when shepherd dogs ran free when the titlark sang free when the wood ibis
waded into the marsh without a care in the world when human beings were less
sadistic when animals had safe conduct safe passage safe haven. across all the
species i am driven. cockatiel, the crow at dawn. mad as a rooster. or fish every-
where in the realm. beautiful from the outside, could you know me inside. may
I know myself? what is the mind of an animal? what does the animal dream?
what does the springbok dream? the spring chicken, what does the spring

chicken dream, or the springer spaniel, what does she dream. what does the vinegarroon dream? what does the falcon the quagga the razorback dream. the rattlesnake? what do they dream. is it a dream of predation and sorrow? is it a dream free of care? what do they dream? what is it to be locked in a bleating kind of ignorance where you have no recourse to sanctuary where you have no recourse to justice? where you have no time to be in any other kind of mind? when you shut down and do not vote you cannot make a choice because you know not the choices you have been fixated on the basics too long. & the wit it takes to survive "person" but your astrologer tells you what you are: queen for a day. mad as a rooster. restless as a monkey. you are linked to the animals in constellations of them, further afield in a cosmos of animalized spirit-drama. as human projecting "i am animal" survive to tell you, it is a realm of blinders on a realm of no recourse to choice to privilege. acute senses, ranges of perception make it harder. physical abilities such as coordination make me suppler. i look into my own mind and reflect what is seen. better not seen this haunting animal nature but in imagination in legend in fractal time.

Where to lobby for it? Identity
All animals in the void hungry for it I doubt
Any finch that knows its name
And that is nothing we can fathom
Body parts mangled in the real nightmare
Of a life buying gasoline, queuing in line
For what's on next
Be careful these days
All the days of our lives
And plurals the hot word to come a long way from home
Diminutive it's not or is it? in this prologue-catalogue
Of seance and meditation
Of science and invocation
Speaking of a rambling woman will
Walk another continent in search of herself
To meet these stones, to meet these stories
Let me tell you a story
Always trace origin, the dance hall long closed, what swagger you relish
A state of suffering from discarnate personality
Where can you go now, the spot shut down
Dance? coins? drinks?
Even money going strange
Will fun be gone?
Where can you go in your world of renunciation
The palaces and sites the shrine
The mosques the citadels heavily guarded
From beta decays from the bestial kaftan
She is a name I recognize
The taxi driver from Solo Christian down to his boots
This is a man I knew in *consociational* time
A side café? A stick of meat
A little bag of nuts,
I knew once, held in sweaty hands

Sweet almonds as I listened to the Pope pontificate
Once in the square of the fully-armed Vatican
What other memories of Church and State?
The Hindu memory
Worship of Kali, Durga
The Sufi spin, the shun by male priests
All are offered here
And speak of cloth and sugar offered here
As you might offer at a Balinese wedding
Sweetness and shelter
It is in verb noun adjective pronoun full sentence with clause you must arrive to
It is in gerund parens I prove my point, or my comma
begs all the marks you must arrive to
Life's in the sound you can make your own
Wouldn't you say to yourself life's all and all how it *sounds?*
Like Mantra you arrive to and repeat ad nauseum
Til it's part of the fabric all our days
Want a node to shift
Want you the other voice (of stupa) to speak with me
Then interface spoke you are my abstruse knowledge
Flip side is illative, knowledge itself
Shift my load to my word
Like: My influence comes from the hieratic the divine you want to,
like, fight about it?
Huh not shifty enough?
Huh not "straight" enough
Academicus horribililbilityus
(I made that up in fury)
Mave somlethinbg up?
Illum immum I remembert illium I sing

India iliac I remember I sing
Java jiltlick I remember lilac I sing nonsense syllables
Inebriinquisitonaris vanadium mixus
You want to know your enemies for sure
And lie down with scholars and saints
Every girl leans on a saint for a while
You want to master rugs and guns under your skirts, no?
They use words like "war" like "challenge" like that
Freedom thing, you know that freedom thing?
She said, spitting out the word "demoncracy"?
Go demonize the sound the way the girls would
Gossiping as they stand on oak leaves
Fallen from the tree by the school library
One wore a little peace sign around her neck, another a silver cross
Digressing from my walk now, another a crescent moon
Mind on the other continents as they fall into place on the map
Is it really one world? I doubt it
A planet for your thoughts . . .
For these were the discursive thoughts
On my trek through Kedu Plain
Sleeveless jerkin
Human mind, animal mind
Nonconformist creeds
Every girl changes the pronouns of herself
And I am one of them, girl and pronoun both
And I am one of them, woman and pronoun both
Yearning and waiting for the opportunity of a lifetime
To best advantage
To seethe and writhe in dust
These were my thoughts of "I," "she"

human realm (beyond your norm of watching)

Wanting to communicate all she heard all she understood, in her meanderings so far I want to tell you this human lore story of all about The Rose-Apple Island Jampudvipa which is a view Indic in origin of all she understood about how that there are four continents situated in the cardinal directions around Mount Meru of which this one this nurturing one called Jampudvipa is the one, a glorious one a pretty one a rose-scented apple-scented one a pleasure garden a pleasure dome a mountain of verdure, also known as a planet as an Earth as an abundance where everything is gleaming and even more lush and nurturing than you can imagine, and integrated and crystalline and at night too, starry and celestial so powerful you are magnetized to a state beyond your norm of watching waiting looking that the very state of the beauty of what some call a firmament what some call a splendid creation some call a mother earth some call a miracle some call a "it could once be that still again" if as those some say you understand time is a spiral, imagine it in its nascent violent and beautiful time past which is now which is still happening light the light that takes so long to get here is over it is still happening imagine it in its dawn of civilization time, imagine the first languages in first language time—Sumerian, Akkadian and Eblaite—which were related to the sounds of birds and animals when the connection was not lost on which we the humans of this time and place dwelt with our moon and with our stars and with our sun that is finite and will go out some many many moons from here, & other planets we might still be discovering because it takes the human eye to note to notice to name to tell of it over & over naming and telling all about the way the human being realm where we live is beautiful is sincere is trying to be in communication with all the animals when we could do that, when it was an imperative when they—the animals— were our spirit helpers when we could talk and warble and spit and hiss and bark and howl and be fully human because they—the animals—were the mediators, the interpreters, the sensuous all-knowing ones when it comes to proprioception when it comes to a kind of hidden nascent understood yet not vocalized ABC language when it can be at its best not be arrogant keep moving to the next thing beyond accomplishment and all about how it stands alone in the cosmos or multi-cosmos of a view of many islands many "earths" if you will, many other places where Buddhas do or do not dwell inhabiting all ten directions of space and time out out out beyond what you could even fathom although the human being has a mind all about meandering about mulling it over about connecting the dots about many the synapses that build and sway not just something in the mind but something in categorical time and space something that can be tested can be measured and may be made visible to the eye or to the magnified eye or the eyes of a thousand lenses, a million lenses. And when we say speed of light we say this as humans. Light is our survival, warmth of mind never lost in survival-thinking, no more likely to be spent in the realm of configuring, in the realm of easy money in the realm of no questions asked let it all be gone by the boards so that no one gets hurt no one gets exposed no one of thinking beyond to thyself be true, moving into realms of empathy and remorse. I wish I had been. And what do they go on. Take pity on anything you harm think no harm—the animals, the trees, the greenery and humans, and so on. You are human so you can think of what they may be feeling to be "other" or if they think that way confused no not really more it is the case it is the very admirable case of speaking it is what you think it is and then the didactic purpose it is. How many citizens died in this week of September this year is known. Think about it. 16,000 innocent civilians. That is the curse no that is the blessing of the human realm to think perpetually beyond. Beyond the tower marketplace beyond the border of enemy and invader, beyond the border of your own desire. What does it bode weird human definition more than a token of getting to one place and another, over and over. I was distracted here I went here I was so distracted everywhere I couldn't actually sit down because there was a realm over and beyond this one. Come to the campfire children. Are you a phony, are you are you standing in the light of the corral. The latter no "dis" in Tibetan distinction. Each line contains and don't we mind humans between doubtful typos to differ.

I've tried to recount the "human" here for you
You know the ear is not always hearing words
as they are spelled and written out here
Is it even your tongue I walk in, citizen?
This was a dawn to describe such phenomenon
This was a dawn entered without pretense
The past tense was all it took getting here
The little room in Yogyakarta bare bulb I love
The men most of all only men I could see
saw me as pilgrim or missionary with hennaed hair
My white socks my ample skirt
My prayer beads my sturdy walking shoes
scholarly books, dark glasses
Talking not talking but murmuring mantras
To communicate (restless hands) to communicate
Devotion—palms together in *anjali*
Saya namanya Anne—it's no matter
With a mind so restless, mind too hermetic
Like cosmetic in pencil form much used
Or drawn out, twist then conclude turbine agreement
on the mouth, cubistic thinking, and rouged angel face
Who to roll and secure?
Toe, heel, lift the other leg etcetera
Who to sell furniture I mean solo
Give up all worldly possessions?
This is the kind of thought you have, pilgrim
Who having lamelliform antennae
And lane news, news of all the traffic lands
Are not exempt from ignorant trifles
Fossil fuel, fossil landforms

All the airways and their sad securities
Sad how dangerous we are in knowledge
Let me tell you about walking meditation
Heel toe pause lift heel toe pause lift
When a government rest house that stood next
to the stupa was destroyed during the Indonesian revolution
Archeologists were able to study the site and
unearthed hundreds of potsherds and bronze nails
Pavilions must have stood in the area, they kept working
A large bronze bell came to light, kept working
Ninth century gold ornaments came to light
Including a finger ring with a stylized "sri"
Marked on an oval bezel
Fragments of statues—more fragments of buddhas
Heel, toe, pause, lift—come to light
Surgery with heart exposed all like a dove aflutter
Dominated by the need to survive
Like danger in the ten commandments of love
Get real says someone, like love is attachment
Birds are real, the real magpie is just one example
Get on knees to speak to doves, crows, robins, stellars, phoenix
And the lamb is a kind of bird
See the structure? Rising up before you
Also: four ceramic jars from the Tang period
Two grinding stones, a 3 pronged bronze *vajra*
A bronze halo
Are you closer coming closer to your
Own secret nature
Animal teeth, kitchen middens
Pottery made by beating wet and malleable clay

Relics abound here
Bases, ewers, dishes, lamps
Stupikas, votive tablets stamped with Tara goddesses
In twenty-one colors. Two rolled silver plates
Inscribed with mystical formulae called
Dharani, which were meant to be chanted out loud
(Tibetans believe a person may become "lord of the tenth earth"
by reciting *dharani* over a stupika)
One lead-bronze plate contains the term *mahavajra*
Or "great thunderbolt"
Observe the worship of Hindu gods in the shadow of the stupa
Observe Muslim overlords in the shadow of the stupa
Observe the syncretic brew of the phenomenal world
You hope you survive the heat
Pages burn—touch the picture in stone—
one technological world's buddhafield as you pause to think on it
an imaginary rift—
That child I watched last night was a little dreamer
Coming out of the womb of complication
I write this now because I fear the end of nature
For your life, art and mind in stone
I fear you could perish
I know I will perish
Stormy waves of birth, old age, sickness and death
And take a vow in aspiration to record a passage here
Blunt, the clause (cause)
Blunt, an effect (affect) But keep telling my life it's a tribe
taboo too, a way out of suffering
Un-fix identity, disarm the hour the people the context
Look up!

warring god realm (distressed god gossip and suspicious eyes)

See back of all the hidden corners. Everyone is the "me my own the enemy." Everyone is "O you ministers & Robber Barons of Death," everyone is "O you Traffickers in Body Parts & Bank Notes of Death." Everyone is looking at you from behind your back the *agent provacateurs* of desire behind your back, backing you up. I say I have eyes in the back of my head, eyes in every pore. I say I have probing eyes to "take you out." I say "Cosmos Positioning Machines to monitor every mood swing." I say "Thermal imaging devices to spot you six miles away at any time of the day or night you better come out of your cave your nook your cranny your crack dope den your crevasse your secret planet or stop hiding your missiles behind the moon and take the heat." I say all this. Plot a moment maintain this dangerous "a" moment, secure the building, fix the opponent, measure the progress, take the heat. Language is a game: a distress: a war: a game. Language is a quill-in-hand-performance. All the particles of desire in language could make you name the weapons in space, relative or absolute space. All corners are suspicious and distressed in my distressing language of dominance and oblivion. See you through all the corners of all my distressed warring god gossip and suspicious eyes. Eyes in every suspicious pore. See me see through my red/green eyes See me continually monitoring you through my cold/greed eyes. You will never get the jump on me, golden, who is there first oppressing you with preemptive motion, preemptive erotics of distressing war motion to make the first move: fair trial? Never. To you who have authority to demand records from business, bank, credit unions, pawnbrokers, car dealers, casinos, consummate genocide, I say "Where is foreplay?" I say this in my Destructo Swarmbot Voice, in my Robo-Bug Voice. I say "Fuck me don't Fuck with me" in my Gnat Robot Threat Detector Voice. Don't play games with me who sees all the hidden corners out of all my Robo-Bug Eyes, all the suspicious preemptive moves. I am extremely efficient with my proud Destructo Swarmbot Jaw with proud face to show you accuracy in every cranial blow I administer. I say I sing I am resolute in moil and toil. In "occupational progress on the ground." I say I sing my Mingnangkabau song, I say I'll sing a patriotic cannibal song a transformative get-down-and-grovel-deportation song. I sing of Warfighter, of orbital imaging and surveillance of arms and no man. Of arms in space and no man left behind and no man in space when we can launch our kinetic energy rods, our oxygen suckers, our happy suppression clouds, big deal cluster satellites, holographic decoys, sexy microwave guns. When we will launch our 360-degree sword-mounted displays, our pyrotechnic electromagnetic pulses, our searing flechettes. Space O I sing so of Space the injured Dharmakaya Space, the sweet relative Space! Everything capitalized and romanticized in the German Noun Space in American Empire Space and in the ultimate High Ground Space, the tower from which to pour boiling oil, I say "Global Battlespace Dominance" I say "Full Spectrum Dominance" and pour more boiling oil. We must, O earthlings, have the ability to control the high ground of space with our Hyperspectral Subtle Light Signature Observation Device which distinguishes a field of oats from a field of barley and tells you the specific species of oats and whether the field contains—is it natural? or genetically altered—oats? And whether the field is infested with insects or damaged by nitrogen depletion. And tanks under trees. I sing thus in my Holographic Battlefield Deception Voice of "tanks under trees." I sing O sing of what will be no space left behind and we'll be able (suspicious-eyed) with our distressed Robo-Eyes in all the corners of our body we'll be able to discern the unique light signatures of extremely specific things like tanks resting under trees covered in camouflage or tanks painted with a paint made to make them *not* look like tanks resting under trees. So if the bad guys are hiding tanks under trees and you have a good idea of what the bad guys' tank is like and you know what the local trees look like then you can screen out the trees' wavelength and just see the tank's signature. Then you'll know if there's something bad under that tree and you can bank in Spectral Light Ray Scary Library and oats of infinite space and time. And barley time. I say I sing "we're just putting another arrow in our quiver." And you can spend your days imagining how an enemy might exploit space because it is our manifest destiny to exploit space and it is a dangerous world out there.

One pause before an age in eternity for it is eternity here
Did I say that? The warring god mentality replied
Corridors, corridors the more weapons we make
The merrier . . .
O the life and the little dramas wherein there are life
O the life and the little stamina where in *sturm und drang* quite
eager to be light and in safety dwell
Beauty is born within and beauty your conundrum
Who holds a woman in esteem here is my friend
Not hieroglyph nor language nor "ur" stone fought turf
I remember of zenith zilch my sweet inspiration an aspiration
Jump off the wheel no one left behind
Boddhicitta, a tender heart for all this cunning
Who holds a woman in esteem is truly my friend
You are the thoroughbred horse
Somewhat reactionary and somewhat well-trained
You begin to like the world around you
And enjoy the projections outside of you
Jangchup-kyi-sen is your state of mind
Jang means "purified," "cleansed," "cured"
Chup means "absorbed in" or "possessing"
Kyi means "of"
You have quick reactions
Taking the bodhisattva vow is like buying a ticket and reserving the seat
Made to moan woefully of suffering
and guide the renunciants into submission
No, that's not it . . . you want to walk free
And to aspire to circle around the pages
stone remonstrances, stories in stone
stone libations, a world of wondrous stone . . .

See on the horizon there?
Are you and you are almost there, little person
one pace one thought at a time
Silent valleculas, quiet vainglory,
silent in a need to reiterate reactions,
tremolos through time. Hesitation.
Why are you here? Toe heel lift pause
Of free accord. An art that is site-specific
Coming out of aloneness
An only place to be
and many might speak thus of
a vocabulary of intention
To speak if such a thing man-made could speak
and one lifts aspiration as one circumambulates
block by block to wonder who made this
who speaks because of this you want
to hear the character and all of them in tableau vivant
demonstration in performance imagination is
a shiny key too to what moves and walks
all the particles and also conceived this of
what we might be capable of to speak many tales
many composite lives in allegorical complexity
by allegorical day by allegorical swelter
of one planet among a vast sum of cosmological proportion
It is a long story every man every woman
every planet's tale and mighty too in invention,
in inclusion of Hindu Muslim Christian Jew, Tribal, Woman, Wicca
and all the animists composite things and
beings too the animate the inanimate
and so on the trees the greenery and so on

and those who live somewhere between
not one gender not one site not one station of life
not one border behind which you are tortured
on the other side queen of your world not one
slip (careful, caution, caution but don't tarry
don't tarry) to hinder you in your progress
and so on, nor monument built here sumptuously
all to see not one dogma not one sentence in a perfected
grammar only, not one habitual pathological tendency
stop gaze walk wonder contemplate bow
perform ablutions other rituals other chanted formulae
not one longing to be lauding it over anything
or to let the better view get the best of you
the trees are there—the mangroves, royal palm
an intelligent seed-idea once left this trace behind—
you look up, look back, a guide
taking pilgrims thru the Six Realms of Suffering
such a sweet gaze toward them
and so on so you build a text of stone
and travel beside it as parallel universe, walk stop gaze,
study the reliefs, panels of more aspiration
a picture worth a thousand words?
and so on, dream slowly slowly, walk slowly
mind don't tarry so the pictures speak a hieratic tone,
keep the wall to the right detach oneself
from the miseries of the world not really
you feel them, heart open forever to others' suffering
recurrent cycle of cause and effect
slowly moving up the labyrinth
the Kedu Valley far below

god realm (of jasmine of anything you want)

what occasions this. . . . wanting the phenomenal world to suck me off . . . suck me off all day chasing the dragon rock 'n' roll . . . pleasure given status, give me service, give me inebriating elixirs, give me promises to prolong all pleasure, prolong all glittery glint of silver screen mythic fountain, of youth dream pleasure. no lamentation no remorse no conditions but that which services my pleasure. no tongue no ear no eye no nose no body no mind no cessation of emptiness no emptiness to work against but this frozen mind in time, my supreme ultimate solipsistic pleasure of suck-off-time. no coca plants no sucking up to you to get nowhere, no speech no sentimental speeches please no more just normal sex but radical sex. the seat gets hotter in the trophy home. no more dialectics, critical theory just suck me suck me take me to the pleasure dome in the middle of nowhere where you've got a cerebral portrait in the attic you grow younger by, no. . . . I mean. I mean what is a god and why am I not one of them? no . . . come sundry one and all after you suck up the utopian Kubla Khan night & of jasmine anything you want I would give pleasure to. I would pleasure you in the seraglio of jasmine . . . where without duty & its orifices, one can lie in lien to *other* because what irks the relation of god realm to other? *absorber/absorbere* =suck. incorporate no source of anger no bad news nothing wanting help in calibrated time. just suck up the pleasure. god lost track of god-time. completely pleasure-oriented to blow no whistle on the dangerous cartels of corporate sex-world-god-time blow no whistle on the gilded palaces of despots, the harems of despots, the torture and rape of women in the gilded halls of prison despots. and down under too. hope and fear gone away down under I lost them—those memories—in my noblesse oblige obligatory god realm. beyond hope and fear in noblesse oblige god time. suddenly you have become a maintenance person, a service industry person to push karma. become shaky person important person with looks like a god pushing your good karma that got you here so cherished, so fawned upon so sucked up. but that is what your bliss was trying to tell you about and thought if you could just try the Olympian mode you'd be exquisitely happy with the new toys they've got for you. but the continuity strangles the holiday and you will only fall down. movie actress hey they say she's only a "B" when he was confused about the end of the Lotus Land story. simply can't go on without a movie goddess to take to bed. judicatorial consent proffers the role. then to give in becomes manifest so we are in an ultimate zone of deranged smoke. we and the quite permanent god of mountain realm will suck up out of this hookah the more of which to enhance pleasure of all the orifices. of we the hole in which analogy our own silk suffocates itself. poof! it goes. poof! a black hole. a mouth. a sucking sound. goes into glutted materialism it does, although I wander through thick black fogs of materialism I still aspire to see the loved one's face. shakes you into a sudden mental fix which creates the self consciousness of the dweller the speaker of all houses of he who strains not to lose ego but lost track of ego's intelligence. and melted down. atomic bombs which bind which suffocate which kill could rouse a god for a day perhaps, but he closes his eyes, sleeps a long *kalpa*. a sudden violence has been cheated of the sex act. you condemn a realm and cheat its seductive fear, an opiated moral torpor forming more seditious hope. venture our capital adventure. the whole point is in stepping in now (you get tired of this realm & are restless) to penetrate the next womb . . . thereby jump into a new place of birth. now light the light (*strike the gong*) and around we go.

mystery — the spread of Buddhism across the eastern Iranian world + then shamanistic pre-Buddhist Bon which originates in a gesture toward Persia — in Tazig, early paleolithic —

mystery — Bon religion in Zhang Zhung, kingdom in Central Asia near part of (Iranian) Mt. Kailash during 5th century BCE. Iranians came to N. Tibet! wheels + wheels of synchronicity

mystery — Buddhism preached in neighboring India (from abt 2nd century BCE — 6th century BCE) as an abstract philosophy, no god at its heart, expands on bigger scale 2 centuries or so after the conquest of the Middle East by Alexandria. This expansion coincides with the rise of a new East Iranian empire established by the Kushan who thrust deep into India — (interchange between Indian + Iranian worlds — more research)

mystery — Buddhism extended over most of Afghanistan (only called such in the 18th century). Culture thrived around 200–1900 BCE in the northern lands around the present day town of Balkh. Civilization of Elam in the ancient kingdom of Shoosh (Susa) and Anshan extended from Southern Iran to much of northern Afghanistan.

mystery – how Iranians coming down from Central Asia intermingled with Buddhism – how it seeped deep into Iranian lands eventually extending over most of Afghanistan, much of Tajikistan, Turkmenistan and parts of Uzbekistan.

mystery – translation of an 11th century Persian romance "Vargeh and Golshah" whose idealized sense of "beauty" echoes Buddhism – trace? memory? Beautiful boys celebrated as "Moon-faced Buddhas" with almond eyes, arched eyebrows, tiny mouths
Buddha figures on sites across Afghanistan... Hadda, Kabul, Ghazni – to the valley of Fondukistan and Kunduz

mystery – A whole Persian romance in rhyming couplets was composed by Onsori, an 11th century poet from Balkh under the title "The Red Buddha and the White Buddha," which were the names given to the two Buddhas in Bamiyan, blown up in March 2001 by the Taliban
there was a sacred third "shadow Buddha"
                              lovers there?

and from the later Song period traces remain showing that pilgrims continued to visit Borobudur after the court civilization had left central Java...

The Hidden Foot: Mahakarmavibhangga

*[Being the series of instructive reliefs buried
when architects went to re-think, re-figure the plan
of Borobudur
and started over . . .]*

Beneath the surface of any action
any dialectic where we get civilized
till earth, make crops grow
any drama any crime engendered
any sacred or profane ground
any marketplace, any pleasant hour,
any muddy path, the road least taken
Beneath gleam of a lantern,
Underneath twilight,
lies proof: traces of
Evidence—
Picture this: objects of farm culture—shovels,
cutting tools, backhoes—
& maritime culture: boats, sails
rudders, masts
& fashion culture: earrings, necklace, a scarf
quotidian life of business—a stylus for
accounting
quotidion realm of "charm" things to
make spells with
quotidian life of crime things: plot & strike, shock & awe
Picture something scenic and its opposite
Picture the way an evil mind works
Cunning or desperate
A person grasps the lover of another
Regard the pang and power of jealousy
Demented it grows
A reason you might kill "over" someone
You didn't get over it
Would you kill over him? over her?
Would you kill him? or her?
A change of scene: not worth it

But still a location of events
for harming others
Picture a suicide bombing
Picture: retaliation
Picture: exploitation of land
Exploitation of someone else's suffering
Starvation exonerated far away and how
nobody did anything about it
It's too late: revenge
A whole generation of revenge
Observe: a nationalistic war
A war of cultural difference
Working some poor fingers to the bone
in the *maquiladoras*
Closing in on the survival of endangered species
Turn a blind eye to
Condone killing a blind eye to
No intervention
Standing by when another partisan species
is wounded or maimed
Time is an arrow
Comes back to haunt you
Time is a "defining moment"
The time is now, strike now
In all good time
Keep good time, don't kill time
Don't squander time
Look, she said, they are coming for you
You were tipped off to the Internet Police
You were set up for a fall for not paying taxes
Your file was opened, your phone was tapped
There was no hiding place down here in cannibalistic time
Justice? Penance?

You are no Titan
You can't do it all
Can't find any purpose any-blooming-where
You might be consigned forever as an eater of toads
if you go on behaving like that
You could sit on Death Row
You could be innocently wronged
while others walk free
if you go on behaving like that
You might not understand any of the
languages around you
You may lose touch here
You may be tainted with the chemicals
of poison and slow death
if you go on behaving like that
An extreme response to a minor action
A conditioned response call it?
The eyeball pierced with innuendo
A thought reversed, eyeball gouged out
by a dangerous weapon
if you go on behaving like that
Armament manufacturers will rot in hell
What can we do now?
Picture this: humans cruelly flaying each other
(old hand to hand combat) then atoning
for their sins in *Sanjiva* hell
This is a hell where creatures tear each other
with bare hands decked with iron nails
while a terrifying bird with a metal beak attacks them
if they go on behaving like that
Don't murder innocents or
you will be repaid in *Rauvara* Hell
impaled on the metallic thorns
of gigantic trees (if you continue like that)

Picture this: bird hunters are
condemned to walk thru
the Sword Tree Forest where
leaves drop from trees and stab them
Cooking fish, you cooks are thrown
into a cauldron (*Pratapana* Hell)
If you are a slayer of sheep your hell
is to be sawn
in two like a magic act but there is
no connivance here
For smoking out rats, you will be crushed between rocks
in *Sangheta* Hell
A system of sub hells plays out before you,
how cruel will it get?
Walk on grass-like spears or
water burns
or you could be trampled by elephants
What have you done?
Did you kill something today?
In the human realm? In the animal realm?
Did you bomb a multitude, take out a country?
Will your punishments turn you into a bird
a four-footed animal
a ghoul next time around?
Matricide: a very hot hell
Say it again: very very hot hell
Genocide: a hotter hell a most hotter horrific hell
Inscriptions guide you, carver of stone
To put these concepts to picture:
"deformed, ugly one" "heaven" "bell"
"village chief" "king" "covetous"
"evil-speaking" "false creed"

what about "future" "buttock"
"flashback" "luminous" "Luddite"
what about "relinquish" "holy war"
"sorting office" "sortilege"
how about "thrash" "thoughtwave"
"undercurrent" "dissent" "crusade"
what about "algorithm" "alienation"
"adultery" "cryptanalysis" "download"
"malodorous" "sputter" "transpontine"
condemned to vermiverous Hell?
covered with boils and blisters in contagious Hell?
To the carver of stone: we wait for you in the hot sun
to relay the urgent message which to all our worlds
(Islamic, Hindu, Buddhist, Koranic,
Christian, Anglo-Empiric)
equals pain
Be careful
Avoid all negative action
Do not move against our faiths
That creature's life is rare, is raw
Do not lift a hand in the name of a false god
Social democracy could possibly guide you astray
The stakes are high
Jean Luc Godard might enter here
with a snappy ironic slogan or gesture in red
The past is in ruin
The bourgeoisie won't stop shopping
The war does not bode well for anyone
The heart is missing from the contract unless it
is for the victims of attack
Where were you the day we fell down?
Prefiguring one says, or in our lives?
An inflectional formative payment of debt
A scepter'd isle of class and race
Where were you?

Subordinate beings of the United States!—where are you?
Citizens and intellectuals take heed
—where are you?
Empire as a way of life?
And what is the punishment for that?
What is the punishment of Late Capitalism?
Exempt from what sordid adventures?
Time running out
Dante's hells also heating up
Enter the holy stupa mountain now
Not Cheyenne Mountain they could destroy
all life from, NORAD's Mountain of Doom
The scene of this research is a way back
out of severance
Pradaksina—a ritual circumambulation
to wear all karma down
If you do this to this this happens
Dancers drinkers molesters:
Keep the writing on the right
Shady groves in the left-hand path of your mind
Around around around
in a "mission: civilization"
Keep the writing on the left
Nations no longer narrations?
Ki Mas Dana fought nearby
Many rebels died
Whereupon it is said Ki Mas Dana fled to
the "mountain Bara-Budur . . ."
the "Bhumisambhara budara"?
Prince Pringga-Laya and his troops pursued him
They surrounded the mountain, captured Ki Mas Dana,
and sent him to Kartasura to be executed by the king.
But mountain of a thousand statues so strong here . . .

Wanted to tell you a story:
How the Javanese descended from seafarers who
left the south China seacoast some 6,000 years ago
They travelled a chain of twenty mountains
and were traders along the Silk Route
The Chinese monk Faxian 400 C.E., went to India to obtain scriptures
and returned home on a merchant ship via Java 414 C.E.
Prince Gunavarman of Kashmir
Yijing of China in the 7th century
chanted the Jatakamala out loud in Sumatra,
and offered prayers to Nagas
Sarva Durgati Parisodhana—
(sang the elimination-of-all-evil-rebirths text)—
The seeker arrives on top of all this history
See the Warrior in a cage!
The seeker says "I came to see the Warrior in a cage"
and stretches a finger inside the cage of "Kacek Bima" at the very top
Wooden carts drawn by bullocks hauled the stone
iron chisels, hammers, chimed in on a natural hill
taking more than sixty years to complete
then fell asleep for a thousand years
You must wake up
become Lady of the Tenth Earth chanting your *dharani,* your spell, over a stupa
Stories are what explorers will say about the world
These are some stories I walk among

Nations are narrations
Spiritual sites are narrations
Ineluctable witnesses to other narrations
are the panoptic meditators in their own bell jars
Ancestral curves keep spiraling of narration
Distance from here to there is a kind narration
Where are you on your global positioned map
as you seek narration: why were you born
& what is your job in narration?
Will you be seen at the top of the mountain in a
trajectory around and around of narration?
Leaves . . . a vendetta . . . how to enact purification or
punishment in a miniature of narration?
World of stress and strife
crosses a culture with a strange philosophy
with a religion you could go dreaming by
across a culture with a grievance
A Neolithic one?
Time's span is from dear Neolithic
Trans-history, trans-humanize
Rapacious to be thus so human
And then I went away from here,
dazzled by the light of a seductive realm
of cattle
of stone
of gender
Elegaritarian generosity, had they?
Doubt?
Pastoral niche, surely
And then I . . . I might doubt it
A long project ignoring frictions
Fictions of generosity
Palette and brush announce this to you

A connotative splendor resides here
And then you come back to some small
votive instrument again, playing it passionately and singing
hyberbolic praise for this path won't win any takers
Pathopoeia might win a few
Apoplanesis won't do it all the time
yet you keep playing
Interruption may be an unguarded
suspenseful moment
To the barbarous world say this: Don't Step On Me
I will create the most subtle philosophy & song
ceremoniously attended to by intellect & intuition
origin & meaning
But we know so little
but Allegory
Transient and fragmented
Redeemable by this mental book as in
Allos, other
Agoreuein, to speak
It is a fable of identity
A representation that interprets itself
Pride for the rural nomad who settled to build, to found a city
You'd better carry your virtue on your back
Get unencumbered by worldly goods
Are you attached to a woman a man a child a household
To thy own self?
Are you attached to
opening a bracket on purity
of the beauties of Narration?
A bucolic interlude of lost luggage—are you perplexed by it
Or just scared?
Thus have I seen
Thus have I heard . . .

One might cling to depression
but you should know better by now
One might cling to romance
but you should know better by now
The intervention of science might assuage your tears
but you should know better by now
You might hold out for utopian transcendence
but you should know better by now
Don't falsify the common world
you should know better by now
One might cling to an ideology
but you should know better by now
One might walk away at one moment and live to regret it
but you should know better by now
Coquettishness gets you nowhere
but you should know better by now
Taut reasoning, what is forbidden
what is revealed?
Know better, you should, by now
Lost in the realm of curiosity: *Abhidharma*
Thin note paper—what did it say?
Some cryptic handwriting not meant for you
you should know better by now
Harsh tones from the leader's speech
You rally against—they got your number
but you should know better by now
Being used in the name of beauty, nuance
you should know better by now
Bowing to flattery, addicted to response
To the adulations of the crowd
You know better than this
A false note at a critical moment

When the trial of your best friend could be
a blessing to you
you should know better by now
When wielding of power could be a boon to you
When all hope fails
you'd better know better by now wouldn't you think?
A light in the window not for you
you should know better by now
The discovery of tricks in the trade
you should, you should know better
Falling into a syncline
you should know better by now
Worrying your uniparous child
you should know better by now
Make time stand still you can't do this
you should know this
a doubt in the mind
you should know better by now
One might fault the fractured steps, the broken path
but you know now you keep balance, a measured gait

Drawing of Borobudur by F. C. Wilsen, ca. 1850.

Jataka Mala (Garland of Births)

[These are some carvings of birth stories called the Jataka Mala originally written by a man named Aryasura in the fourth century, describing the praxis of self-sacrifice]

On meeting a starving tigress the future Buddha
(who is currently a hermit)
gives up his body as food
His relics are worshipped by gods

Indra comes disguised as a blind man
Buddha who is presently a king gives him his eyes
and Indra returns them,
happy with Buddha's noble act

The future Buddha is head of a merchant guild
He and his wife have to pass over Hell—
a seething cauldron with humans in it—
to give food to a monk

Indra steals the material possessions of Buddha
now posing as a rich man—
Buddha becomes a grass cutter
living a more modest life

A future-Buddha-as-rabbit teaches his friends—
otter, ape, jackal—generosity
Others bring food but the rabbit
jumps into the cook-fire

Buddha has himself cut up for ogres
and as a prince gives away his prize elephant
He is always fussing for others
Going the extra mile, he is too good

His people tell the king (secretly Buddha)
that the only way to assuage a drought
is to conduct animal sacrifices. When he
says no, sacrifice evil humans! *everyone* behaves

Gods and demons are in battle
and the gods are in retreat
Future Buddha as Indra turns abruptly to save some birds
And the demons get confused

Although he falls in love
Future Buddha won't accept the beautiful woman
proffered by her husband,
He doesn't want to generate more conflict

Merchants prevail on Buddha—a former
ship's navigator, now old and blind
to lead a journey. The ship is
blown off course by a fierce squall. What next?

Future Buddha prays for safety
and the ship resumes course
Rocks and sand retrieved from the ocean bottom
turn into gold and jewelry in the crew's hands

Buddha as a fish prays for rain: it comes
Buddha as a fish prays for rain: it comes
Buddha as a fish prays for rain: it comes
Buddha as a fish prays for rain: it comes

A young quail—our noble Buddha—
eats no small living things. He halts a forest fire
by praying to the fire god
Renounces the world to live, human, as a hermit

His companion Sumukha refuses to leave his side
when Buddha-as-Swan is captured by a hunter
The king puts them both on thrones
The hunter bows down

Ascetic Mahabodhi—Future Buddha—
a favorite of the king—argues
with the jealous courtiers after falling out of favor
and proves their doctrines erroneous.

[Nidana Chain: the Twelve Images: The Wheel of Life
1. carrying the precious sweet body to the charnel ground
2. mother & child: the arising of a thought or mood in the mind
3. existence: sexual, as in copulation
4. picking fruit—grasping
5. thirst—liquid—offer a drink?
6. sensation—man pierced in the eye by an arrow
7. contact—this with that, you name it
8. six senses—a house with six windows
9. name & form—boat filled with passengers
*   form is the body of a boat moving on the river of life*
*   carrying aspects of our being—all those personalities*
10. inquisitive monkey
11. a potter making pots
12. old blind woman]

what is a lesson about heroism about deeds?
and why does the heroine escape from the palace to the sky
looking graceful, the posture of her arms and hands?
what are the deeds of pilgrims of seekers of
dreamers that lead us to higher ground
how do these deeds benefit others
what is sacrifice, valor, fortitude, bravery
what does "virtu" signify?
what does stalwart, gallant, courage or mettle
mean to this time, fragile dark ages, the Kali Yuga
why does she move so beautifully in stone?
a valiant knight, a knight in shining armor,
a paladin, a demigod who are these actors?
and why are acts of heroism so bound up with
lives of other species in acts of confrontation or love
why is a human crossed with a bird?
why does it take the snake charmer seven days
to lure the serpent *naga* from its realm
why does the *naga* traffic with people
in the first place
what is the attraction of *nagas* to jewels
why does one want a *naga* in one's kingdom?
what language do the animals speak and
how do we humans communicate
why do we pick on animals for our heroic deeds
what does "rescue" mean?
when we were closer to the animals
were we any the wiser?
and why are men invested
with the job of heroism so completely
& women become the objects of heroism which are
shuffled and bandied about and exchanged
and captured and bartered and raped and sold
in the lore of heroism?
lovely Manohara gives the *naga*
a jewel from her own forehead
and is completely in his power: why?
what is a talisman of bondage

what is a *naga* doing with a bird-woman to barter
what does the watery realm they
inhabit signify, what kind of allegory is this?
what is the hidden meaning behind *naga* behind
a deed of seduction, the lariat that binds her?
when Monohara the *kinnari* goes
back to her own kind is she happier?
when her own kind try to wash
the stink of the human
off her body, is she happier?
do women have their own will in any of this?
what kind of halfbreed is a *kinnari*
in being half bird half woman
what does that signify?
what is the bird-in-me-as-woman
that I move like a bird, Leda
that I think like a bird, Leda
that I follow certain migratory routes
oviporous
that I am soft with downy feathers
does it take a prince to save a woman?
could she save herself?

And what of this other story—
A king drinks fertility water
meant for women
and gives birth from his forehead to a son
who grows up to having the gift of
Wishes-Come-True
He wants to make life easier for his subjects
showers of grain and thread fall from heaven
at his command—
seeing that his people still have to weave thread
whole pieces of cloth drop now
then gold falls for seven days into his chambers
He grows greedier and soon plummets from heaven himself
Or this—
A woman follows her leprous husband into exile
Indra rewards her virtue, heals up the man . . .
And this—
A king from Benares comes upon a *kinnari* couple
weeping and embracing
They had once been separated one night by a flooded river
It is said *kinnaris* live a thousand years and although
this had happened 697 years earlier
they still regret their one lost night

. . . was . . .
In the mouth all sound
Denied in night & then
Hell, no! out out
A breeze towards lines of philology
Lines of philosophy towards cohesiveness
Towards traces of pilgrimage
Air gets in being humble
The word gets in the marrow
Being mantra
OM AH HUM
And a place to visit gets in
Being humble, also holy
You might propose
An offer of poetry
Recited as jewels in a lotus
As you turn (body) turn (speech) turn (mind)
OM MANI PADME HUM

Might be a sound easy to offer
Linguistics: state of grace
OM TARE TAM SOHA
Easy to consider goddess Tara
born of Avalokitesvara's tear
Wheel: perpetual riddle
Myth of the weapon is
objectifying it as a turn
around the block for a
gorgeous pointed thing
It must be used!
So said the jaguar
in another religion
in the great debate
that signaled "war"
A heart sighs "bodhicitta"
"bodhicitta
& signals "come back"
to haunt you—back to compassion,
to the negotiating table

NOTE: *Religion exists on earth as the fuller*
form of the eternal art of poetry . . .
It works like poetry which bonds
to the Infinite putting off the Indefinite
into most holy forms of thought. . . .

—paraphrase of John Milton

The Avadanas: The Narration

[chanted]

Let me tell you about
Crown Prince Sudhana of North Pacala
and the beauty Manohara . . .
Two fans: one of peacock feathers, another of leaves
rise behind the king and queen who hold court . . .
A conch is their flower vase
A *naga* my dear sea serpent, dwells in a lake of the palace
The grounds are fertile
South Pancala's rival king is harsh, cruel
The country is dry and barren
As he goes hunting the king of this realm passes through many deserted villages
No *naga* will bless his realm
A reward for anyone to bring a *naga* to his kingdom
A snake charmer weaves a spell to lure the *naga* from the other kingdom in
seven days
I can't resist, the *naga* says, the music is too strong but a hunter Halaka who
lives beside the lake will help him

In return for help the *naga* gives Halaka a magic lariat which will always snare its
prey

The hunter captures the nymph Manohara—half human half bird denizen
She is completely human here on the stupa wall
bathing in the lake

She gives him a jewel from her forehead, signifying that he has her completely
in her power

The prince passes by on a hunting trip and the hunter offers the nymph to
him. He falls in love and rewards the hunter well. They marry.

Two brahmans arrive in North Pancala, one becomes the king's priest, the other is
promised the position when Sudhana inherits the throne but the first
Brahman is jealous
and convinces the king to send his son into a dangerous battle

The boy gives the jewel to his mother saying *Please guard Monohara during my absence*
Sudhana is shown in audience with the queen making a gesture of respect
Courtiers hold flowers, fans, regalia

Sudhana wins in a battle some kind of rebellion with the aid of forest ogres
The king asks the wicked conniving priest to interpret a dream which in fact
means success for the prince but the priest interprets as requiring sacrifice
of a *kinnari*. The queen learns of the danger to Manohara and allows her to
escape by returning the jewel to her hand

Manohara flies away
She doesn't want to abandon her prince and gives her ring to a *rishi* telling
him how she can be found in the country of the *kinnaris*

After returning victorious the prince sets off to find his wife, gets the message
of her whereabouts and enters the *kinnari* kingdom

He meets nymphs drawing water who tell him it is to be used to wash the
odor of the human realm from Manohara

He drops a ring into one of the water jars
And of course they find each other

Her father wants to kill him but relents and requires him to pass two tests. In
the first the prince must shoot an arrow through seven trees and hit a golden
post. In the second he has to identify Manohara from a large group of nymphs

How would he know her?
He just does
The pair are reunited
Other dramas? Other dreams? A king drinks fertility water meant for women
and gives birth from his forehead to a son . . .
This son eventually Prince Mandhata banishes some holy men who cursed
birds for disturbing their meditations . . .

Indra disguises himself as a falcon and chases a dove
A virtuous queen follows her leper-husband into exile . . .

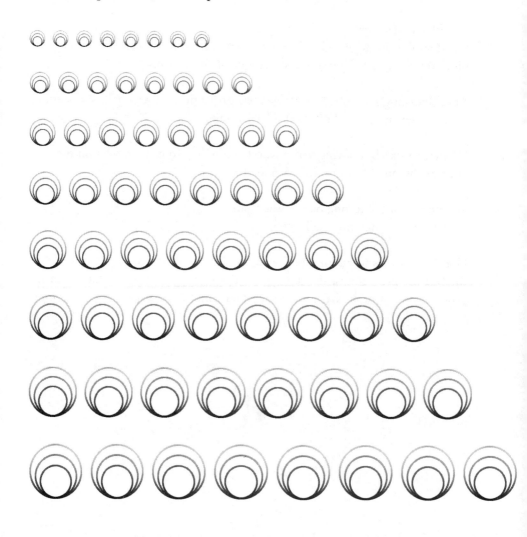

first

In this stage the adept is you
Adapting to the place you are, the spot you are
Adapting to the structure of your own commerce
Start here. A dot in space
A first place of "put forth" and "put out" and staging
a "set up," a scenario
For all these plans and runes, these guises
You are magic! you expand
You are never crumbling. You are magic!
You are ready to purchase your ticket
You've got it all worked out
You are sitting beside an old friend
You are trying to say goodbye but you never have to
You are magic! You do *both* all the time—
saying goodbye, never leaving
You understand the dual-nature of "gain" "saying"
wherever you are, whether under a gun,
or under a restrictive government
Whether you are off looking at the gibbous moon or
you need stamps or you have crossed the desert
or the well runs dry, then it rains
A ballgame is consuming, yeah
because you think too much. All the moves
are on your mind so that
you appreciate manliness,
noblesse oblige, now that the slavery
of sports is capitalist, pandemic
revealed and exposed for the big business it is
I want to buy my thrill and that player can be worth a billion
if he needs to be, gifted and stunning
He can play until he drops, or she can
No this is starting out with pity
Nothing as tough as that
No big attitude about that
Life is cheap so you think: renunciation
No it's not like that

You are weary of wanting anything
to cheer you up or
entertain you
You aren't in shaman training exactly
with spell-making
You want all sentience to shimmer
to shine
You are not trying
to be an officer holding a weapon
or ecclesiastical officer holding
a writ, or drama queen having a fit
You officiate for yourself
in polyglottal mode
inside your own asteroid belt
not injurious to anyone
taking them with you
a kind of shuttle in space
Your metaphorical ring is caught by
a metaphorical hook
You are the loop at the end of a lasso
Let down the beautiful hook with the rope
in the jailhouse now
Up out of the oily greasy turbulent ocean
of a topsy turvy world
The ring and the hook meet
It's a state of
raptu gawa
Which translates as
"extremely joyful"
Sounds like rapture
Sounds like awe
Myth becomes reality or
dana paramita—literally
arriving at the other shore
(with generosity)
This first level or headline is of generosity
Generosity of material objects:
candle, medication, warm clothes

Generosity is the transcendent fiend
A flashlight might be a transcendent friend
Security is in the mix and
drunkenness is in your generosity of
a first level bodhisattva
But no hangover
A neck resists the rope
She wants to be saved she can't
be held by a rope that's a kind of hook
What kind of hook is it that
metaphorically saves you?
Now reach out to me . . .
Dutch *hoek,* the old colonial power
bent back at an angle for catching
and it bends towards you, but it's
all a different sort of dream

second

This is a weird translation
Bottom, thou art translated!
sila parmita beckons you
patiently out of dream
and the level for this kind of
aspiring action is named
trima mepa
trima means "spot" or "dirt"
and *mepa* means "not"
so this is the purity or spotlessness
discipline, not-dirt! not-spot!
Obsessive!
any germs you collected
are being purified
How interested you are
in how the world functions
independently of you
How the world functions
is as a message each time
I was thinking of the new streetlamp design
Is it too industrial?
Deaths in Somalia and our country's
complicity there
Thinking of ways to repair the stoop
Thinking the gestalt of the Siliguri station
the old court gamelan
gong deeply resonant, ancient woman plays . . .
Try to guess her religion: Balinese Hindu or Muslim?
Elements on the street before you get to the noodle shop
(stoop slightly to go under)
I was thinking of how
you are never off guard
even when nothing happens
Everything that happens
is an expression of dharma
And a bodhisattva does not

become a maniac in this view
You are working with sentient beings
because you are interested in them
You have ceased wanting to conquer
the world as image
And put all things in their place
as Heidegger's *Vorstellung*
(The bringing forth and setting before
the subject of all things) would
It's that simple

third

Conjure *ojepa*—*o* means "light"
Jepa means "creating" or "activating"
Manufacturing light, producing light without being tired
The paramita *kshanti* or *zopa* means
"endurance" or "patience"
With each level you are approaching
the capitol where the highest civilization exists
You are coming from a small province
You are approaching from the frontier
where things are not all that sophisticated
A *shabnamah* brought down from the hills
urges you to fight the infidels
As rivers get closer to the ocean
they become larger, while you feel small at first
A slow expansion takes place
Are you wondering why I tell you this?
I wonder also because life is difficult
And the world's in flames
At dinner tonight we discuss all the atrocities
from Sudan to Iraq to Afghanistan
Indonesia in a holding zone
How much instability can you create
in one miserable year
Legal brothels in Canberra better, but AIDS on rise
Hold mind, your ground, stop exploiting women
Are you one of the privileged?
Discursive thoughts on the dharma are encouraged
But not going too afar
Let's jump. Make it a leap. A brave plunge
Let's not shift the scenario to a field yet
The ultimate distraction: room with a view?
Head for the watering hole

fourth

Otrowa means
"radiating light"
which celebrates
tsondro, the paramita of exertion
Don't be afraid of anything
I will never take off this suit of friendly armor
No indulging emotions no entertainment
Immovable exertion
Your mother is dying your child is small
From diaper to diaper
Keep cool
Free from pride

fifth

Difficult to accomplish: *jangkawa*
because objects and what you think of them
become necessary, brilliant
confusing in their presence
and you are apt to solidify your thoughts
about them—
how they work
how they "appear"
What do we think of them and of people too?
One thought for the ancestors
One thought for commemorative buildings
Decisions on hold for those neo-con statues
One thought of an elaborate (iron blue)
listening device and you'll be accosted
by it, maybe a subtle sense of comfort
haunts you
which then cultivates knowledge
meaning there's enough space to be sane
Meditation in action: again, again
Working with other people
and performing miracles
but not turning oil into blood
You still haven't recovered
from your own experiences but
others become more important than you at this point
Try to teach, try to work with them,
Be generous toward them
You seem less blind now, psychologically speaking

sixth

Experiencing reality
referred to as *ngontu-gurpa*
you experience numbers, grids
directions, study maps of all kinds
Where are you? What is your number?
Can you drive there?
sherab or *prajna* is the crossing over
Without the eyes of wisdom the
five paramitas are like the blind wandering nowhere
but *prajna* (wisdom) is the linkage
so that you could have
appreciation of people writing poetry, shooting movies,
people paint pictures, it's okay to be an artist
as children make a dance go on & on in twilight
like that: words on a page or strike a dissonant chord
or collect knowledge
"I love you" is one kind of terrific knowledge
but this bodhisattva is analogous to being a mountain
You have no beginning no end, no middle
A million becomes zero

seventh

The bodhisattvas march forward
with diligence and effort singling out
ringtu-songwa meaning
"far gone"
We visualize the whole thing
We come from a continent and we see an island
We try to sail across to get to it
Then crossing the island we take another boat
Is it our endless journey or quintessential journey?
No boats to take anymore,
no trains, no scary airplanes
We've crossed the island and the mainland
of the samsaric world
"Skillful" means
wanting to want to
tell you this: nowhere to go
Not separate from the body
or called back from trust as, like, omigod my pretty body
Part of your body, not separate like a knife
An analogy is that the strong medicine taken in internally
becomes part of you
Not an embellishment to prove your
masculine or warlike quality
Knowing one's own weakness is skillful
and then knowing the other person's weakness
as a need for your application of "skillful means"
is another apt means

eighth

The eighth step
(step faster now, catch my breath)
is called *miyowa*
"not moving"
This is a paramita of aspiration or inspiration
a resolution to hold one's seat
Usually you approach outer space or a foreign country
and begin to panic
but bodhisattvas don't ever have to think of strategies
They just arrive
and are immovable
and are a good friend to the dreamer
with their permanent visioning devices
not giving up on long term projects:
the one hundred year project
the 2,500 year project
undoing plutonium
whatever it takes

ninth

legpi-lotro
means "good intellect"
You are smart about
this only game in town
meaning mind and its machinations
hooked to all the sense perceptions
Power is the paramita,
power of fearlessness and the power of rejoicing
Those exist without having to conquer the world like
a wish-fulfilling gem—
It's a sweet non-flinching quality, no jitters
You put your jewel (an emerald, a pearl) on
a specially prepared shrine (amrita, incense, musical instruments)
You ask for whatever you want to happen
but it must benefit others
in the immediate present
avaunt disease!
save the child!
You tell all that to your jewel and in a few minutes
those things happen
in your magic lantern of mind

tenth

cho-kyi-trin:
"cloud of dharma" is
the last stage of the bodhisattva experience, a final
step before the attainment of so-called enlightenment:
jnana
Ride free from psychological hangups of all kinds
(fear of tall buildings, fear of space, fear of glass)
that could exist in the realm of
samsara or even subtler samsara
In the earlier stages the
bodhisattvas still have something to go on
something to develop
—scent of what realm?
This bodhisattva sees the world in a very brilliant way
So bright it's like the vision of a full moon night
and strife is as an empty bottle of perfume
There is no prostrator, no object of prostrating, no prostration
Offering incense or flowers to the shrine only exists as a reminder
as the place of worship bounces back on you
Not worshipping an idol
demand comes out of the shrine itself
"It" becomes a personality
Shrine is a field of merit
Acknowledging what you have done your whole life
and your weakness is a kind of adoration—
Adoration for a greater vision of the awakened state
Request the dharma teachers to stay alive!
Share your merit!
Dust your shrine!

eleventh

kunto-o means
"always luminous" walking back and forth in
vajrapamasamadhi—vajralike samadi
Knowing and seeing, holding a
diamond sword, back and forth walking and knowing
knowing and seeing
and cutting through
the two obscurations:

1. *klesavarana* (belief in a solid "me")
2. *jneyavarana* (objects of experience are solid and possess independent existence)

Gautama Buddha took seven weeks
to grow confidence and a sense of
being articulate. He sat down, he sat still
He spent one week gazing at a *thal* tree
Then walked back and forth, forth and back, along the Naranjana River
Once you are a buddha you have to proclaim:
Wake up! This is possible!
And mention Bodhgaya where he sat under a tree
Stand up again

The stupa walls spoke of Veranasi where the first sermon took place

[Discursive thinking as a ground core melody, punctuated cyclically by gongs, Borobudur at dusk]

◎ It was dusk
◎ And she walked
◎ Silent as she reflected
◎ As silence
◎ Might speak
◎ To speak if it could
◎ Silence refracted
◎ Could be said
◎ To circulate
◎ In blood
◎ A carving in stone
◎ To wonder
◎ And Buddha spoke
◎ Block to wander
◎ Sun gone down
◎ And a block to
◎ Speak
◎ Walking as if
◎ In a city
◎ In a sanctuary
◎ Under metaphorical *ficus religiousa*
◎ Reasoned out
◎ By augur: to walk and sit
◎ In a sanction of this place
◎ Which is blocks of pictures
◎ Blocks of stone
◎ Or a forest
◎ Blocks of trees
◎ Every allegorical
◎ Woman
◎ Wants
◎ To be a pilgrim
◎ Wants to bend and be

◎ Holy in a landscape
◎ Wants life in fact
◎ In truth to
◎ Be a journey to a mountain, to a forest
◎ To a park
◎ Towards some place you may rest
◎ You can let go of who
◎ You don't want to be
◎ Every woman wants to be
◎ Built for strength & for suffering
◎ And to submit not
◎ To anyone who might have
◎ Built her up for this
◎ A woman says
◎ For a parallel, observe "things as they are"
◎ Built for a Universe
◎ One she helped build
◎ They as things are
◎ And made to sit with animals
◎ Buddha might be a woman
◎ Buddha is the woman
◎ She thought
◎ Thinking to herself
◎ Because she felt she could
◎ Emulate a buddha
◎ Slowly step right, masculine principle
◎ Slowly step left, feminine principle
◎ Slowly keep walking beyond gender
◎ Slowly make a turn and woman will pause
◎ She will stop
◎ To study the details
◎ Of the ancient city
◎ Right now detach
◎ Heel . . . toe . . . breathe
◎ In step with the *Belegangur*
◎ Old Javanese "walking army" music
◎ Eyes would close in on
◎ One another, pause she takes

◎ Now before a stone
◎ Mohammedan middle
◎ Of my life
◎ Mohammedan moon
◎ A moon around the pages
◎ On which you might
◎ Scribe impressions upon
◎ Spears, stones, religions
◎ Little animals sweet in repose
◎ Can such a thing be created
◎ Man-made, ha! and harmonious?
◎ Hasidic moon
◎ Easter moon
◎ Sanskritic moon
◎ Woman hauled and cooked
◎ And provided sons
◎ The house (& daughters)
◎ Who made it!
◎ The boss from
◎ Beginningless
◎ Time—ha!
◎ Is many tales
◎ Many composite
◎ Adventures I
◎ Will tell you some . . .
◎ Every planet's journey
◎ Could end up here
◎ Inside her cellular dream
◎ The inanimate the
◎ Animate and so on
◎ To see and so on
◎ Walk and so on
◎ Speak and so on
◎ Stop gaze and so on
◎ Walk slowly, leave the safe palace
◎ So we understand you better
◎ Keep moving up, upward
◎ Before the

◎ Book-world and so on
◎ Stone remonstrance
◎ Could never
◎ Won't be silent
◎ What's the otherwise?
◎ Point of proclamation?
◎ Allegorical planet
◎ Among a big illusion
◎ We are serious beyond Patriarchy
◎ We are sweet
◎ Even in our
◎ Crazy death
◎ Dying for a religion, no
◎ The trees the greenery
◎ I said gender not one sight
◎ One sound
◎ Gender you light up build a text
◎ Upon
◎ Welcome here to study
◎ Relief, the truth of suffering
◎ Pictures speak of relief
◎ Of one misery
◎ All shared glory
◎ Of horrible tortures
◎ And deaths
◎ Of poverty and famine
◎ Of mental labyrinths
◎ Attachment to all you love
◎ One book says
◎ This is libation
◎ This is transmigration
◎ When you wake up & face the music
◎ A long man a long woman story
◎ A story of persons
◎ Children
◎ Adepts
◎ "Lineage"
◎ & transgressed because in love with phenomenon

◎ And all lies and truths
◎ Between
◎ All the debases of existence
◎ And your databases of existence
◎ Stop from being holy and
◎ What is holy
◎ Without ego? Everything!
◎ The inherent nature of all phenomenon is pure
◎ My own nature is also pure
◎ A hieratic tone keeps the wall
◎ To the right
◎ An endless circling of tortured
◎ Thrilling cause and effect walked through this

some say the heaven of contentment but I say it is right here in a secular paradise—perfume of flowers, millions of instruments, a cord around the waist—for a mystic pose . . .

some say his mother to be . . .

some say, some say it is a Buddhist dream

enter from the east, what form to take? an act or motion of moving of stirring mighty thoughts like who are we what are we doing here what about suffering what can we know what shape of a life can we be might we take to be the most effective inside this world system if you had a choice what life out of all the lives you could maybe inhabit possibly take would you want to be inside of that would give the most succor the most delight the most ease the most joy the most relief the most support would it be that you would have the life of a teacher of a wayfaring stranger a benevolent ruler a healer a medicine man a singer of songs a judge a station master a mayor a musician a holy woman a rebbe a mullah a meditation "master" a philosopher a poet a dalai lama?

propelled by "goodness" you could say, the thrust of taking shape to "walk among" the interstices of the suffering denizens in the suffering world who have no perspective on old age, sickness, death, who think they can take "it" all with them, or that they are immortal or that they can kill others, the enemies, without karmic consequences . . .

"enter the stream," then disappear from the world, like this one buddha of this one time did, our time our historical version of historical time did, a time propelled by a benevolent consciousness that moves to do the least harm, to eradicate harm . . .

notice four directions of the compass

1. to interweave the events and daydreams of someone's day
2. a vessel, or a bridge, a particular form to walk upon
3. winds, inclement weather, high tides, full moon, sunspots
4. conversation or love affair with the phenomenal world

& this is the sermon of the deer park, the wheel of the law, that one would not have to *suffer in the mind* so much one who arrived once was coming in as buddha was showing up in the appearance of buddha he was not a saviour not your particular salvation not descending from on high not reigning down from on high not born to be a martyr not born of seed & egg not born as a deity not born as a god not a fool for love not a fool

Maya in a forest of asoka trees dreams the elephant enters her womb

as if a splendid elephant with six tusks as if enclosed in a golden tent, as if enclosed in silence and in giving birth maya illusion is the vehicle and this as a dream, the buddha before he is buddha is bodhisattva Gautama not a real person but an identity assumed to help people reach liberation and this is as a dream how one is tested as in a fairy tale as in an allegory using an ancient bow preserved in a temple sends arrows through seven trees and one iron boar, simultaneously as in a dream as in a tale cuts hair, puts on robes, leaves it all behind a lotus grows from the ocean a lotus that is the essence of all creation Brahma collects the essence in a lapis lazuli bowl and gives it to buddha to drink and in the birth saga part takes seven steps in each of the four directions of a compass and this unfolds as a drama so you see how a life is played out inside the pleasure garden many women to entertain you everything at your beck and call while women slump in sleep, outside the gate: guards drowse to allow our curious prince to get out there, leave home, get out and about and see an old man dying

buddha in performance enacting a lot of different guises and selves, buddha as an historical perspective relegated to strange lore, to magic, buddha before he was buddha studying a femur or other bone analyzing how life comes to be, in this case buddha thought: "life comes from death" buddha becoming a convenient animal but an animal that was special and ready to die for others, buddha as a baby elephant, buddha outside the harem, buddha taking steps out of the womb, walking out his mother's side, buddha formed from systems and patterns, buddha on the tip of the tongue, buddha of signs, symbols, or gesture, buddha as document

how many gestures towards a buddha that is sitting still, that refers to a lexicon, that refers to desire, buddha as text, buddha as dogma, buddha as jargon, buddha as a subculture around which people bow and prostrate, buddha as something that is only in the mind, buddha as a particular utterance in an old dialect, buddha a kind of identity

gong:
gong:

GONG with accoutrements:

Slit Gong
Holy Water Vessel
Naga Spout from a Holy Water Vessel
Rattle with a Coiled Serpent
Temple Bell with an Ox and Trident
Hand Bell
Top of a Bell in the Form of a Demon King
Top of a Bell in the Form of a Kneeling Demon
Top of Scepter
Hinged Box in the Form of a Tortoise
Chastity Plate
Pair of Ear Ornaments with Ram's Head Motif

Structure of the World Compared to a Bubble

Our youth Sudhana ("good wealth") sets out for wisdom
sets sights on wisdom and what is that?
a chimera, a phantom, an idea, a generous thought
a way to not get stuck inside his head, mulling, stewing
plotting the end of his enemies
a way not to pick up a weapon and do some harm
He's the story of just-a-curious-boy-could-grow-this-helpful-way
He's the protagonist of a circular story of repeating visits
to spiritual friends
& mystical visions of benefit to others
He moves along but how does he travel
He seems to be walking, now he is in a sedan chair
An elephant will carry him
& a carriage
It is like a movie when you may stop and start and dream
and start all over again being tracked by an omniscient eye
and shimmering forms repeat and beckon and thoughts grow
more abstract imagining beautiful places
He is transported by his mind
Maybe he would make a wrong turn and learn something
He is our Parsifal or our Candide or any woman
For one instant
his lips
slowly press onward—ask a question
if he did falter
chilliness of the night
imagination: a guilty platform
for one instant
if he did falter we think he would persevere
not fall from the precipice nor lunge under the juggernaut
a kind wind for any storm
what is it to travel in a forest such as this
up among the clouds
motions reach the space
warmth by day
where your thoughts are just comfortable clothes to wear
Sudhana sees the Buddha in a garden in "the appearance of the lion"
Eyes bulging, hands and claws extended

Buddha with celestial beings in a forest
uncompromising and strong
He meets supernatural teachers
Buddha Manjusri and Bodhisattva Samantabhadra
and Maitreya, the future Buddha, who will be his guide
Life is strange and inspired and interesting
when the mind wants to travel between "this" and "that"
Some of the students cannot see miracles happening
because they only seek salvation for themselves
as when the Buddha becomes invisible, throne gone empty
and one has to give up a conditioned way of seeing the world

or when eight goddesses appear in dreams and awaken people to announce that someone has become enlightened or when Maitreya opens the allegorical palace with a snap of his fingers or when Maitreya conjures his jewel tower replete with flags, bells, garlands of cloth, pearls, nets of gold, songbirds, and you linger over a lotus pond—just there, see it?— reflecting your basic fearless nature . . . . or when we see all of Maitreya's past lives and we see Maitreya walking without stopping for thousands of centuries and we see Maitreya discoursing on the artistic and scientific ways to benefit all sentient beings for thousands of centuries giving his own body to feed ogres, setting prisioners free, treating a sick child, showing the correct path to lost travelers—they are so weary—carrying a friend across a river wounded in an old atavistic war and we, the pilgrims, we who have our Good Youth traveler stand in for us on this path in this allegory-dream you could say we inhabit the heart of Sudhana which is akin—this feeling in heart and mind—to the feeling of a person in a dream in a helpful dream where the conditioned things of this world (a hard cruel murderous time) disappear and what thou lovest well remains a kind light a sweet light shining through conditioned time then climb up, pilgrim, climb across time for thousands of centuries more and more abstract and into a future of what shape will that be? what world within worlds within universes whose neutrino-light travels back and forth in sacred conversation no stopping it in the future now, space empty of manipulation how luminous how luminous now . . .

    touch crust
visualize

        mantle
over
core

            magnetic/gravitational
pull
of core's
courage cover

you are my theory of the earth centered upon itself

oxygen/silicon
            smoky quartz upon itself

a crystalline vajra stone

& the agates along this coast
are the eyes of the Rigdin kings

what

to   do

with

the

          hands?

all ten thousand of them
   made
     visible to save the world

risible
no received ideas no things
but what you witness *in things*

          all sense perceptions
as witness
or palm down
     as if to say
you are my earth & will witness me

roll

       under your scrutiny

right hand's
    palm up: charity?
native sagacity
inclined to an

untamed forest

merry women we are who

    tithe the rich please,

no more

tax cut

unawares to have thought
    the mind in
tumult to
        kind intimacy

        sphere of matters private & otherwise
        save the environment

& creatures respond in "cut" to be taut
    an old *chod* practice down the mortal line . . .
      "cut" "cut" "cut" "cut" "cut" "cut" "cut" "cut" "cut" "cut" "cut" "cut" "c
        "cut" "cut" "cut" "cut" "cut" "cut" "cut" "cut" "cut" "cut" "cut" "c
          "cut" "cut" "cut" "cut" "cut" "cut" "cut" "cut" "cut" "cut" "c
            "cut" "cut" "cut" "cut" "cut" "cut" "cut" "cut" "c
                "cut" "cut" "cut" "cut" "cut" "cut" "c
                    "cut" "cut" "cut" "cut" "c
                        "cut" "cut" "c
                            "c

halt, fear
fear was not abiding, says
the tide is turning, says
justice will be had, says
understatement, says
the poet the prophet and the priest all say this and Manjusri says this
"all is well"
all 504 life-size buddhas flashing mudras, say this
"all is well":

Vitarka Mudra: *listen, thus have I heard*
Dharmacakra Mudra: *turn the wheel quickly*
Dhyani Mudra: *deeper in contemplation,* go, go
Abhaya Mudra: *halt, fear*
Bhumisparsa Mudra: *touch the earth, witness our beautiful planet*
Vara Mudra: emanations of generosity
(scent of *tamalapatracandana* arising here. . . .
  Tantrika
    flailing

at the top
    of oneiric abstraction

"Bowing down" as cause was always mysterious in its playful insistence on being the most obvious way you could do something rash or not so rash once you set your heart and mind and will to it. Sometimes it was a grievance to be played out agonizingly slowly, paced, over time. Accompanied by a slow dirge perhaps, or three part symphony that rises and falls and you are never quite absolutely definitively clear sure etcetera where you are but you do remember the cause of your action because later, at the trial you are asked about motivation and its music. Why did you do this? Why did you sing this song? What did you lie steal embezzle rape murder commit crimes against humanity? I was crazy or I am sorry I thought it was god's will his Armaggedon is obviously not enough or that you had a rough childhood, a rough life, a rough time being the child of some kind of trauma. Or your parents were conservative or hillbillies or of a gypsy tribe even. Even if they were Rom. So your identity gave you cause, right? Is that a fact? What do you say to your tribunal? What cause do you attribute your actions to? That you felt compelled to alleviate the suffering of others and that by doing this you could win support for a just cause, a new political system? An oligarchy, a plutocracy? A benevolently socialist state? You were some kind of revolutionary obviously, I guessed that. A Kingdom of Glass and Wind? I would indeed like something that included poetry in it. I would like something like a kingdom if I could be a queen, she said. What cause, and where is it arising firstly including poetry.

Mantra < Intervention

gongs and chanted

◎ cau–cus
◎ cau–dal
◎ cau–dill–o
◎ caul
◎ caul–dron
◎ caulk
◎ cau–sal
◎ cau–sal–i–ty
◎ cau–sa–tion
◎ cau–sa–tive
◎ 'cause
◎ *cause ce-lebre*
◎ cau–ser–ie
◎ cause–way

◎ cau-stic
◎ cau-ter-ize
◎ cau-ter-y
◎ cau-tion
◎ cautionary
◎ caught!

That was the philosophical existential sociological phenomenological meta-physical allegorical question. But were you so sure these were valid reasons? Maybe it was the voice of an overpowering mother, an angry lover, a retaliatory worker who lost a choice job. And had a family to support. Someone was always sick or tired or needy. So many grudges in a world. That's what you might be asking yourself now as you stop to think about it. What cause? Later you can lie down by yourself no one but yourself in the night when they turn out the lights and think back: this old bone leads back to this, then that came before that and before that. And now I remember what happened before that. Why someone was angry, why someone acted as she did. But then what? What happened before that? You are lying there on the rough or smooth bed for eternity because you can't get back to First Cause. There doesn't seem to be an ostensible beginning anywhere. Did it all just start when we were born? Where do I come from? I am not a replica of anyone else not yet I'm not. Beginnningless time. But there was a specific action that's the point. What made you act? Can't you remember? Maybe you were drugged, inebriated, in love. Maybe you were hungry. Maybe you are trying to shelter or protect someone else through your stubborn silence. Are you warm enough? Can you see any trees outside the window? Are the birds singing? What are they called in this neck of the words? Robins? Night-inggales? Is that spelled with two gs? What is happening at this very moment on all sensory levels? Where is your mind is it still where it was a moment ago? Or maybe this had something to do with a secret discovery around genetic research. That always occurs to me these days because I am not skilled in science I have no understanding no labyrinthean comprehension in the mazes of those little minute causes and effects that make up discovery and yet assume that a lot of other people are having scientific thoughts, actually getting money for research calculating and making fascinating decisions that will affect all our lives all the time. Even as I ride a subway. Even as I sit on a plane uncomfortably when the food arrives about talking to the gentleman next to me; Who is he? Some undercover person? A bank person? A normal person. A saint? Am I safe? Is he engaged in research that will determine the future of "womankind"? Will he be friendly? Will she be so close to me right next to me her head almost asleep on my shoulder mind if I keep the light on as we cross the ocean in order to read because I can never sleep on these kinds of flights? Take a valium my best friend always says. She says that because she knows it might assuage my fear and loneliness and enable me to sleep but then again she says it because she always says it back in times and in my dreams because it is the only thing to say. Take a valium. Another older person will say "melatonin." But what is the science of melatonin and how it works on the pituitary gland changing a sense of time. So taking medication is complicated in terms of the matter at hand—because— remember? Cause, as in cause and effect will go somewhere, will ripen. Eureka! I am not as smart as you. That is admirable. Research that will help someone recover from an incurable disease is admirable. I am against cloning at this point, animals, humans the lady next to you says. Artificial intelligence is sometimes provocation as an idea but it seems like it would be hard to maintain, another machine I can't get a grip on like this computer with the keyboard of another country's language. The "m" is in the wrong spot, there is no ampersand. Once it was Arabic. Now it is Italian. I will hit the keyboard to get some of these accents in. They are the spice of this workaholic game of writing things down. Back to cause in this instance where you—mythical one—are hypothetically under arrest, in a cell somewhere. You tried to get into the country illegally. You put on women's clothing. Now you are up against the death penalty. All you wanted was a story from the front lines. You have to know the customs and specifically the rules of other countries. The language professor was on trial in India for killing a cow in an accident with his jeep. Life imprisonment? You need the best lawyer you can get. What was he thinking as he rounded the car then swerved I have no idea. What causes any accident or Where is the mind? Once I had been dreamingly admiring at twilight the switching of the lights red to green. They were so beautiful up against a velvet sky—light fading—so crystalline, precise. I could have said then and there that this was the most "real" moment in all of existence. I was completely present. It was the night before Thanksgiving in the United States of America, I was dressed up for a play wearing black velvet with embedded costume jewels or specs of mica or maybe the scarf I was told with bits of silver inlaid by the hands of prepubescent Egyptian girls. Then—my mind wandered a moment—and crash, I was hit by a sports utility vehicle. The cops got me to the theatre on time for the opening monologue. Once I was showing a lover (he was driving) a photographic in an old book of a Mayan temple as he drove. I wanted to inspire him because I was happy about it about us. Here—this is: Coba. The little Volkswagen jetted into a hole—a *topo*—both tires burst. Then there was a long journey to recover tires, repair them. We got out on the dusty road with a lot of tarantulas. I tell you it was not a dream. And we got in a car with two very drunk persons and then thinking that this might be the end somehow thinking about how we'd gotten there from the first idea of fretting there arose, and then looking at books and pictures of these fascinating places studying some language, fretting, this particular car driving on this particular road enough to make you crazy really all the connections but I was also saying goodbye in my head to all the beloved family and friends I might never see. Life is fragile, it is precious I love life, I was thinking. I keep telling the men in Spanish to go more slowly. I am not sure they spoke Spanish. It was a back road, a Mayan place. I was an intruder. I was stupid. We needed to get to a tire shop or gas station or repair shop we did finally there was a young very young capable youth who fixed our life for that one day. Maybe luck. Other times it was quick and suddenly the result of an instant response, irritation or something bound up with sports. You know a reaction the way when that home team loses some of the angry men turn off their television sets and beat up their wives.

Top view of Borobudur, showing the mandala-like pattern of the monument.

[Why does your shrine not have the requisite peacock quill?]

A metaphysics of ascent keeps you moving
In one ascension dream you are poised on a pinnacle
(high above the clouds, above the tundra) dressed up
in rattling bone apron, skulls around neck, third eye glowing
in a "fourth moment" of desire and liberation
Or is that a sow's head atop your sixteen-year-old sex-body?
A Vajravarahi emanation severs thought with her hooked knife
without allegiance or confusion
Mind experiences its own nature: empty and luminous
And what are you supposed to do next, missy, old shape-shifter?
Pulses thrum from stars' metabolic clock say
push! push! don't tarry don't tarry, don't tarry you darlings!
you'll be home soon, (please sit down)
And it was thus, my dream of altered me inside the
head was birthed to be unborn: animalized spirit
gives sway to phenomenal world over and over
And proceeds to a place of "stop this mind"—inert, if that could ever be—
rest, stability, unity if that could ever be in a spot struck by lightning
a kind of *enelysion*
Pop illusion of your solid self if that could ever be
Pop eons of struggle and despair you can do it
Thunderbolts chide you to be what you could ever be
Meteors chide you, you are here to disappear!
All the planets with myriad moons chide you
and here the local rainbow is your scarf to wear
Sit down now on the actual spot, *axis mundi*
atop Mount Meru, the highest chakra
atop all sacred stones, volcanic andesite *in situ* here
plus *salagramas* of Vishnu, all minerals extracted
from all ten directions of space & any religion
All hagiographies of buddhas & bodhisattvas
& feminine principle that accommodates
anything you could ever dream, ever think up
up! up! up! up! up!
Does thinking I have to get somewhere
make all the structure seethe & churn with promise?

& how complex it is to climb through
stages of mitochondria
Hun invasion into stolid Huguenot
all that entered in a particular body incarnate
to be aspiring thus—muscle, tendons, gristle, plenty
of multitudinous matter under scrutiny of personal identity
Human birth (don't tarry! don't tarry!)
precious as the *udumbara* flower
blooming once every thousand years

TAT TWAM ASI

And in the middle of the night in the middle of your life you arrive ground transport done . . .

Buddha at your side sitting by in light attire for in smarter mind of yearning in laborious thinking it is his spry will that gets you here danger comes later danger the cosmic joke that you are impermanent the whole turf permeated with scent of change and "ordinary mind," by that meant a magic that is the link to any digression any distraction in shock in hope of imprint, say in the footprint you have made on this Asian continent it's real, right? And tangible? As clothing? You make something happen. See the imprint you have made, then see how fragile it is. Who are you in this landscape—pilgrim or thief—never broached. Wise up. Broach it now, the penultimate question. Pilgrim on one side, seeker perpetua; old saw on the other, louche, orientalist of imagination. Please do and observe that "will" meaning the "force of will" waits to be elevated for slaughter—that whatever will is, is enough for slaughter. Yet War is. Yet shift the mind at war. Generous.

They build these monuments as an aid to memory. What DNA are you? What will remind you to be kind after all your walking, after all your "pilgrimage?"

In the beginning was the center. In the beginning was a seeker. Yet maybe something could happen to you, naked of light in the middle of your life the Kedu plain now raw stars glowing. Trespass here. Symbols on a wall say Stick with me, in the long run, they say. Come in they say: pacify, magnetize, increase, destroy. Me.

Whirlpool galaxy in Canes venatici *welcome here, setting sail*

There is the story of the medieval merchants of Asia who went out searching the restless ocean for pearls. How many oysters would they have to find to snatch the precious moon-orbs? How far out would they be willing to go? Four anchors, the gentle captain warns the merchants, just four anchors, he cautions. Do you want to get into this or not? All kinds of mystical warnings. So they can make up their minds, have choices, think for themselves. Each day the strong rope holding an anchor is cut. So each day they get closer to the deepest part of the ocean. And each day they have a chance to go back. If anyone wanted to quit the first day it would be easy. One could take a small boat and get back to shore. The second day others might have a slightly bigger boat. The third and fourth days even bigger boats. The last day, fourth anchor cut, there would be no more lifeboats large or small. The seekers would have to stick with their journey with their boat with their imaginations with the ocean until they gathered their pearls. How long? How far?

As if you have to justify your "watcher" one more time you just better go back just drop it.

Drop anchor.
[*breath / pause*   ]

        pull up?

By this merit may all obtain omniscience

May it defeat the enemy wrong-doing

From the stormy waves of birth, old age, sickness and death

From the ocean of samsara may I free all beings.

—Dedication of Merit
(traditional)

Anjali—Putting raised palms together in prayer mode.

Barrd—Bard—any of an ancient Celtic order of minstrel-poets who composed (usually with harp) verses celebrating traditional lore, warrior culture. Strolling poet of any other oral tradition, Anglo-Saxon scop, Scandanavian scald.

Bhumi—Earth, stage, level. Usually refers to the ten stages of the *bodhisattva* path.

Bhumisambhara budara—The mountain of accumulation of merit on the ten stages of the *bodhisattva*.

Blackline Hell—One of the hot hells reserved for thieves.

Bodhicitta—Tender heart of awakened mind. Relative bodhicitta, which arises out of absolute bodhicitta (emptiness indivisible from compassion), is the aspiration to practice the *paramitas* and to deliver all sentient beings from *samsara,* out of one's compassion.

Bodhisattva—One who commits one's life on the Mahayana path of compassion to benefit others, returning lifetime after lifetime to help other sentient beings.

Brahma—The creator god in Hinduism, conceived as a member of the triad including Vishnu and Shiva.

Brocken spectre—A magnified shadow on a bank of cloud in the high mountains, often with a colored halo. *Brocken*—the highest of the Harz Mountains in Germany.

Daka—Literally "one who goes in the sky," a masculine semi-wrathful *yidam* (personal deity who embodies the pratitioner's awakened mind) or protector.

Dakini—A wrathful or semi-wrathful female sky-going protector. Dakinis are playful tricksters representing the basic space of fertility and possibility.

Dark Age—The Kali Yuga. The present world age marked by degeneration of discipline, ethics, compassion, wisdom.

Dharmakaya—Body of formlessness.

Dies Irae—Latin: day of wrath. A thirteenth-century Latin sequence obligatory in the requiem mass in the Roman Catholic Church.

Durga—Hindu goddess of death and destruction, usually seen conquering a buffalo.

enelysion—A sacred spot struck by lightning, as named by ancient Greeks.

ficus religiousa—Pipal tree, which lives on air and rain until its roots reach the ground. The historical Buddha went into deep *samadhi* (meditation) and became enlightened under such a tree.

Five Buddha Families—Ways of understanding the positive aspects (wisdoms) and negative manifestations (confused emotions) of energy as psychological makeups in the world. The five are 1) buddha 2) vajra 3) ratna 4) padma (lotus) 5) karma (action)

Four Noble Truths—The truth of suffering, origin of suffering (ego), way out of suffering, the path. The starting point for Buddhist practice.

fourth moment—A flash of insight that cuts through the web of past, present, future.

Jampudvipa—The southern continent or island of the Buddhist world system named after the rose-apple tree. The entire known world was regarded as Jampudvipa.

Kabbalist—One who studies the Cabbala or Kabbala, the esoteric and mystical Jewish tradition first transmitted orally, of which the Zohar (thirteenth century) is the basic text.

Kali—Hindu creator/destroyer goddess.

Karma—Action. According to the understanding of action and result, one's present experience is a product of previous actions and volitions and future conditions depend on what we do in the present. Karma originates from a false belief in ego, which triggers a chain reaction of seeking to protect territory and maintain security. Karma is precise down to the "minute particulars" (in William Blake's sense) of body, mind, and environment.

Kinnari—Mythical creature, half bird, half woman.

Lamelliform—Shaped like a lamella: a thin scale, plate, or layer, as in the gills of a bivalve mollusk, or forming one of the gills of a mushroom.

Mantra—A way of transforming energy through sound. Mantras are Sanskrit words or syllables which manifest the quintessence of various energies, regardless of conceptual content.

Maquiladoras—Exploitative factories along the United States/Mexico border generally run by non-Mexican corporations hiring Mexican laborers.

Mara—From the Indo-European root that also forms "mortal" or "mortuary." *Mara*—death or life-in-death personified, is the tempter of Sakyamuni Buddha who appeared prior to his attaining enlightenment and was vanquished.

Milarepa—Lord Repa, yogin and poet who lived from 1040–1123 C.E. "Repa" refers to the single modest cloth worn by yogins who were adept in *chandali,* or heat practice, in spite of Tibet's cold winters.

Mudra—Sign, symbol, gesture. Specifically hand gestures that accompany *sadhanas* (practices) to emphasize the quality of different moments of meditation.

Nagas—A class of deities with human torsos and serpent-like lower bodies.

Nidana Chain—Twelvefold chain of dependent-origination or *pratityasamutpada*

Nirmanakaya—Body of form.

Om Mane Padme Hum—A mantra or means of transforming energy through sound. Literally "the jewel in the lotus."

Paramita—Literally "transcendent" or "gone to the other shore." Awakened actions because they carry us across the river of *samsara* and are based on *prajna*, or wisdom beyond ego.

Pradaksina—The method of turning clockwise and gradually upward around a *stupa*, described in pre-Vedic texts prior to 2,700 B.C.E. The right hand stays physically in contact with the shrine.

Queen Sri Kahuluan—Patron of Buddhism in Java, Saliendra family.

Rakshasa—A demon spirit.

Renunciation—A state that arises from the hopelessness and toxicity of *samsara*. In the nontheisitc tradition it is said that renunciation is not something you do, but that out of your experience it comes to you.

Rigdin—Supernatural king in Shambhala teachings—principle of leadership for an enlightened society.

Sambhogakaya—Body of light.

Saya Namanya—Bahasa Indonesian, the *lingua franca* of the archipelago for "My name is . . ."

shabnamah—"Night letters" written by the Mujahideen to rouse young men to the jihadist cause.

Silk Route—A trade route through China and India to Europe, along which Buddhism traveled.

Six Realms—All beings belong to one of the six realms or gates. Higher realms include *deva* (god), *asura* (jealous god), and *nara* (human). Lower realms include *turyak* (animal), *preta* (hungry ghost), and *naraka* (hell). Within each realm there is a psychophysical pattern of recreating your experience based on predominant *klesas* (obstacles). Pride (god), paranoia (asura), passion or dissatisfaction (human), ignorance (animal), craving (preta), and aggression (hell). The human realm is the best place from which to alter the pattern, cutting the cycle of *samsara*.

Stupa—Originally a memorial mound which contained relics of the Buddha, later stupas included relics of other enlightened beings. These sites became places of practice and veneration.

tamalapatracandana—A kind of sandalwood.

Tantra—literally means "continuity" and refers the ground, path, and fruition of the Buddhist journey. The ground is like the sky—encompassing everything from buddhas to sentient beings. Path tantras means one can apply profound practices to overcome basic ego confusion. Fruition tantra means you can realize who and what you are, and that the ground was there continuously from the beginning.

Tara—An emanation of the deity Avalokitesvara; she is said to have arisen from one of his tears. She embodies the female aspect of compassion.

Tat Twam Asi—From the Upanishads. Literally, in Sanskrit, "Thou Art That."

"things as they are"—Basic nature, which is spontaneous, unfabricated, freed of habit and ego manipulation.

Vajra—Adamatine, diamond, indestructible, thunderbolt. One of the five Buddha families. A vajra is also a ritual sceptre.

Sources and Bibliography

Fremantle, Francesca. *Luminous Emptiness.* Boston and London: Shambhala Publications, 2001.

Grabsky, Phil. *The Lost Temple of Java.* London: Seven Dials, 2000.

Harding, Sarah. *Machik's Complete Explanation.* Ithaca and Boulder: Snow Lion, 2003.

Hilt, Jack. "Battlefield: Space." *New York Times,* August 5, 2001.

Miksic, John with photographs by Marcello and Anita Tranchini. *Borobudur/ Golden Tales of the Buddhas.* Boston: Periplus Editions, 1990.

Shantideva. Stephen Batchelor, trans. *A Guide to the Bodhisattva's Way of Life,* Dharamsala, India: Library of Tibetan Works and Archives, 1979.

Simmer-Brow, Judith. *Dakini's Warm Breath,* Boston and London: Shambhala Publications, 2002.

Slusser, H. *Nepal Mandala.* Princeton: Princeton University Press, 1982.

Trungpa, Chogyam. *Orderly Chaos, The Mandala Principle.* Boston: Shambhala Publications, 1991.

Trungpa, Chogyam, and The Nalanda Translation Committee, trans. *The Rain of Wisdom.* Boston: Shambhala Publications, 1980.

Waldman, Anne. *Vow to Poetry.* Minneapolis: Coffee House Press, 2001.

Wayman, A. "Reflections on the Theory of Barabudur as a Mandala," in *Barabudur: History and Significance of a Buddhist Monument.* Berkeley, CA: Berkeley Buddhist Studies 2, 1981.

Anne Waldman is a longtime student of Buddhism and one of the founders of the celebrated Naropa University in Boulder, Colorado, where she, Allen Ginsberg, and Diane DiPrima began the Jack Kerouac School of Disembodied Poetics in 1974. She is the author and editor of over forty collections of poetry and poetics, has worked on many collaborative projects with visual artists and musicians, and is a dynamic performer/ singer of her own "modal structures." A distinguished professor and curator of poetry and poetics and a political/cultural activist, she has been associated with the Beat Literary Movement and the New York School as a second generation lineage holder as well as carrying forward the experimental strands of the New American Poetry. She is currently the Chair and Artistic Director of Naropa's Summer Writing Program and is on the faculty of the New England College MFA program. She is the recipient of the Shelley Award, a former fellow of the Civitella Ranieri Center, and a recipient of a grant from the Foundation for Contemporary Performance Arts. She makes her home in New York City and Boulder, Colorado, and travels extensively to other zones of poetry around the world.

TED BERRIGAN
Selected Poems
The Sonnets

PHILIP BOOTH
Lifelines

JIM CARROLL
Fear of Dreaming
Void of Course

CARL DENNIS
New and Selected Poems
    1974–2004
Practical Gods

BARBARA CULLY
Desire Reclining

DIANE DI PRIMA
Loba

STUART DISCHELL
Dig Safe

STEPHEN DOBYNS
Pallbearers Envying the One
    Who Rides
The Porcupine's Kisses

ROGER FANNING
Homesick

AMY GERSTLER
Crown of Weeds
Ghost Girl
Medicine
Nerve Storm

DEBORA GREGER
Desert Fathers, Uranium Daughters
God
Western Art

ROBERT HUNTER
Sentinel

BARBARA JORDAN
Trace Elements

MARY KARR
Viper Rum

JACK KEROUAC
Book of Blues
Book of Haikus

JOANNE KYGER
As Ever

ANN LAUTERBACH
If in Time
On a Stair

PHYLLIS LEVIN
Mercury

WILLIAM LOGAN
Macbeth in Venice
Night Battle
Vain Empires

DEREK MAHON
Selected Poems

MICHAEL MCCLURE
Huge Dreams: San Francisco
    and Beat Poems

CAROL MUSKE
An Octave Above Thunder

ALICE NOTLEY
The Descent of Alette
Disobedience
Mysteries of Small Houses

LAWRENCE RAAB
The Probable World
Visible Signs

PATTIANN ROGERS
Generations

STEPHANIE STRICKLAND
V

ANNE WALDMAN
Kill or Cure
Marriage: A Sentence
Structure of the World Compared
    to a Bubble

JAMES WELCH
Riding the Earthboy 40

PHILIP WHALEN
Overtime: Selected Poems

ROBERT WRIGLEY
Lives of the Animals
Reign of Snakes

JOHN YAU
Borrowed Love Poems